Better Homes and Gardens®

MEALS for ONE or TWO

On the cover: Fresh-tasting **Garden Omelet** makes mealtime for singles extra special (see recipe, page 52). But when the meal is for two, feature **Steak-Lobster Dinner** draped with a delicate cheese and wine sauce (see recipe, page 15).

BETTER HOMES AND GARDENS® BOOKS

Editor: Gerald Knox
Art Director: Ernest Shelton
Associate Art Director: Randall Yontz
Production and Copy Editors: Paul Kitzke,
    David Kirchner
Meals for One or Two Cook Book Editors:
    Elizabeth Woolever, Senior Food Editor
    Patricia Teberg, Associate Food Editor
Food Editor: Doris Eby
Senior Associate Food Editor: Sharyl Heiken
Senior Food Editor: Sandra Granseth
Associate Food Editors: Diane Nelson,
    Flora Szatkowski
Meals for One or Two Cook Book Designer:
    Sheryl Veenschoten
Senior Graphic Designer: Harijs Priekulis
Graphic Designers: Faith Berven, Richard Lewis,
    Neoma Alt West

CONTENTS

†**Cooking for One:** We've developed many recipes in this book to make a single serving (see list at beginning of index), but you can also select for one serving any of the two-serving recipes we've identified as being adaptable. We've chosen these recipes because you can achieve successful results without changing procedures or worrying about critical measurements. To make them for one serving instead of for two, simply follow the directions and cooking times given and **halve** the amount of each ingredient.

Preparing meals for just one or two often poses a problem because most recipes serve four or more. This means that if you cook a large meal, you eat the leftovers for days. To solve this problem, we've designed delicious one- and two-serving recipes to make all your meals fresh-tasting, varied, and satisfying without creating hard-to-use leftovers. And tips for buying and storing food, supplying a kitchen, and planning and preparing meals will help you do the job with ease.

ENTRÉES

POULTRY

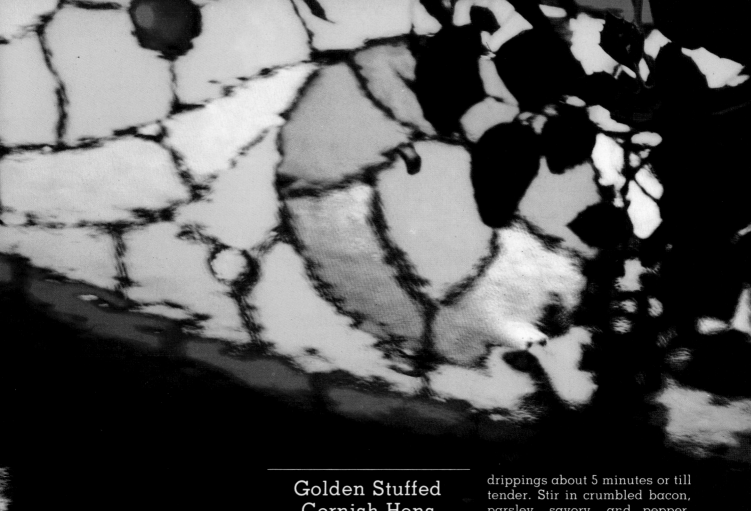

Golden Stuffed Cornish Hens

4 slices bacon
½ cup finely chopped carrot
1 tablespoon snipped parsley
⅛ teaspoon dried savory,
    crushed, *or* ½ teaspoon
    snipped fresh savory
    Dash pepper
1½ cups dry bread cubes
    (2 slices)
¼ teaspoon instant chicken
    bouillon granules
2 tablespoons hot water
2 1- to 1½-pound cornish
    game hens
    Cooking oil
2 tablespoons dry red wine
1 tablespoon butter *or*
    margarine, melted
1 tablespoon orange juice

In medium skillet cook bacon till crisp; drain, reserving 1 tablespoon drippings. Crumble bacon and set aside. In same skillet cook carrot in reserved drippings about 5 minutes or till tender. Stir in crumbled bacon, parsley, savory, and pepper. Stir in bread cubes. Dissolve bouillon granules in hot water; drizzle over bread mixture. Toss lightly.

Season cavities of hens with salt. Lightly stuff birds with bread mixture. Pull neck skin, if present, to back of each bird and fasten securely with a small skewer. Tie legs to tail; twist wing tips under back. Place hens, breast side up, on a rack in shallow roasting pan. Brush with cooking oil; cover loosely with foil. Roast in 375° oven for 30 minutes.

Combine wine, melted butter or margarine, and orange juice. Uncover birds; baste with wine mixture. Roast, uncovered, about 1 hour longer or till done (drumstick can be twisted easily in socket), basting once or twice with wine mixture. Makes 2 servings. (Adaptable for one.)†

†See page 3 for directions.

Honey 'n Spice Cornish Hens

⅓ cup long grain rice
1 teaspoon instant chicken bouillon granules
1 teaspoon lemon juice
¼ teaspoon salt
⅛ teaspoon ground turmeric
⅛ teaspoon ground cinnamon
 Dash ground cloves
 Dash pepper
⅔ cup water
1 tablespoon honey
1 tablespoon butter or margarine
¼ cup light raisins
2 tablespoons chopped walnuts
2 1- to 1½-pound cornish game hens
 Cooking oil
2 tablespoons lemon juice
1 tablespoon butter or margarine, melted

In saucepan combine rice, bouillon granules, 1 teaspoon lemon juice, salt, turmeric, cinnamon, cloves, and pepper. Stir in water. Bring to boiling. Reduce heat; cover and simmer about 20 minutes or till liquid is absorbed. Stir in honey and 1 tablespoon butter. Stir in raisins and walnuts.

Season cavities of hens with salt. Lightly stuff birds with rice mixture. Pull neck skin, if present, to back of each bird; fasten securely with small skewer. Tie legs to tail; twist wing tips under back. Place, breast side up, on rack in shallow roasting pan. Brush with oil; cover loosely with foil. Roast in 375° oven for 30 minutes.

Combine 2 tablespoons lemon juice and 1 tablespoon melted butter. Uncover birds; baste with lemon-butter mixture. Roast, uncovered, about 1 hour longer or till done (drumstick can be twisted easily in socket), basting once or twice with lemon-butter mixture. Makes 2 servings.

Cornish Hens with Cranberry-Orange Sauce

2 1- to 1½-pound cornish game hens
2 tablespoons butter or margarine
¼ cup water
½ teaspoon instant chicken bouillon granules
2 tablespoons sugar
½ teaspoon cornstarch
⅛ teaspoon ground ginger
 Dash garlic powder
¼ cup water
½ cup fresh or frozen cranberries
2 tablespoons orange marmalade

Tie legs of each cornish hen to tail; twist wing tips under back. In 10-inch skillet brown birds in butter or margarine about 10 minutes. Season with a little salt and pepper. Add ¼ cup water and bouillon granules to skillet. Cover and simmer about 50 minutes or till birds are tender.

Meanwhile, in small saucepan combine sugar, cornstarch, ginger, and garlic powder. Stir in remaining ¼ cup water. Cook and stir till thickened and bubbly. Stir in cranberries and orange marmalade. Cook about 5 minutes or till cranberry skins pop. Transfer birds to warm platter. Spoon some of the sauce over; pass the remaining sauce. Makes 2 servings.

Dried Fruit-Chicken Curry

1 whole large chicken breast, split
2 tablespoons butter or margarine
¼ cup chopped onion
1 small bay leaf
1½ to 2 teaspoons curry powder
½ teaspoon salt
⅛ teaspoon crushed red pepper
¾ cup hot water
½ cup snipped dried apples*
¼ cup snipped dried apricots*
¼ cup raisins*
1 tablespoon sugar
1 teaspoon instant chicken bouillon granules
1 teaspoon lemon juice
1 tablespoon butter or margarine
1 banana, sliced
¼ cup coarsely chopped peanuts
 Hot cooked rice

In medium skillet brown chicken slowly in the 2 tablespoons butter about 10 minutes, turning once. Remove chicken from pan, reserving drippings. Cook onion, bay leaf, curry powder, salt, and red pepper in the reserved drippings till onion is tender. Remove from heat.

Stir hot water, dried apples, apricots, raisins, sugar, bouillon granules, and lemon juice into onion mixture in skillet. Return chicken to skillet. Bring to boiling; reduce heat. Cover and simmer 30 to 35 minutes or till chicken is tender.

In small skillet melt the 1 tablespoon butter; stir in sliced banana and heat through. Serve chicken with banana, peanuts, and rice. Makes 2 servings.

*You may substitute ½ of an 11-ounce package mixed dried fruit for the apples, apricots, and raisins.

Bits of tangy apples, apricots, and raisins, delicately spiced with curry, make Dried Fruit-Chicken Curry an exotic entrée for most any occasion.

Chicken Cacciatore

2 whole small chicken breasts
2 tablespoons all-purpose
   flour (conventional cooking
   method only)
½ teaspoon salt
2 tablespoons cooking oil
1 medium onion, sliced
1 clove garlic, minced
1 8-ounce can tomato sauce
¼ cup water
1 bay leaf
½ teaspoon dried oregano,
   crushed
½ teaspoon dried basil,
   crushed
¼ teaspoon salt
⅛ teaspoon pepper
   Hot cooked spaghetti *or* rice

Coat chicken breasts with mixture of flour and the ½ teaspoon salt. In skillet brown chicken slowly in hot oil about 10 minutes. Remove chicken. In same skillet cook onion and garlic till tender. Stir in tomato sauce, water, bay leaf, oregano, basil, the ¼ teaspoon salt, and pepper.

Return chicken to skillet, coating with sauce. Cover and simmer for 20 minutes. Uncover; simmer about 5 minutes longer. Skim off fat. Serve with spaghetti or rice, spooning sauce atop. Makes 2 servings.

Microwave cooking directions: Sprinkle chicken with ½ teaspoon salt (omit coating with flour). In 1½-quart nonmetal casserole combine cooking oil, onion, and garlic. Cook, uncovered, in countertop microwave oven on high power about 2 minutes or till tender.

Stir in tomato sauce, water, bay leaf, oregano, basil, the ¼ teaspoon salt, and pepper. Add chicken; coat with sauce. Micro-cook, covered with waxed paper, 10 to 12 minutes or till chicken is done, rearranging after 5 minutes. Serve as above.

Chicken Kiev

2 whole small chicken breasts,
   skinned and boned, *or* 1
   whole large chicken
   breast, skinned, split, and
   boned
2 tablespoons butter *or*
   margarine, softened
2 teaspoons snipped parsley
⅛ teaspoon dried tarragon,
   crushed
   Few drops lemon juice
   Dash garlic powder
2 to 3 tablespoons all-purpose
   flour
¼ cup milk
½ cup soft bread crumbs
   Fat for deep-fat frying

Place each piece of chicken, boned side up, between 2 pieces clear plastic wrap. Pound out from center with meat mallet, forming a rectangle about ⅛ inch thick. Remove wrap. Cover and chill chicken.

Combine butter or margarine, parsley, tarragon, lemon juice, and garlic powder. Shape into two 2½-inch-long sticks. Chill or freeze sticks till firm.

Sprinkle chicken with a little salt. Place one stick of the butter mixture on boned side of each piece of chicken. Fold in ends; roll up jelly-roll style, pressing edges to seal. Coat chicken with flour; dip in milk. Roll in bread crumbs. Cover and chill chicken at least 1 hour.

Fry in deep hot fat (375°) about 5 minutes or till golden. Drain on paper toweling. (Or, brown cold chicken rolls in skillet on all sides in 2 tablespoons hot butter about 5 minutes. Transfer to shallow baking dish. Bake in 400° oven 15 to 18 minutes.) Makes 2 servings. (Adaptable for one.)†

Spicy Barbecued Chicken

4 chicken pieces
¼ cup catsup
1 tablespoon finely chopped
   onion
1 tablespoon bottled steak
   sauce
2 teaspoons brown sugar
2 teaspoons worcestershire
   sauce
⅛ teaspoon garlic powder
⅛ teaspoon ground cinnamon
   Dash ground cloves
   Dash ground ginger
   Dash pepper

Sprinkle chicken pieces with a little salt and pepper. Place chicken, skin side up, over *medium-hot* coals. Grill chicken for 20 minutes. Turn skin side down and grill for 15 minutes.

Meanwhile, for basting sauce combine the remaining ingredients in a small mixing bowl. Brush both sides of chicken with some of the basting sauce. Grill 10 to 15 minutes more or till tender, turning frequently and brushing with remaining sauce. Makes 2 servings. (Adaptable for one.)†

Use the microwave oven to speed up the cooking time of barbecued chicken. To pre-cook chicken pieces, arrange a single layer in a shallow nonmetal baking dish. Cook, covered, in a countertop microwave oven on high power about 15 minutes. Then transfer chicken to a barbecue grill. Grill for 10 to 15 minutes or till tender and evenly browned, turning and brushing with sauce.

Broiled Apple-Stuffed Chicken, *filled with a tasty apple and herb-seasoned stuffing, is an economical main dish that uses the whole bird.*

Chicken Livers Veronique

¼ pound chicken livers
1 tablespoon sliced green onion
1 tablespoon butter *or* margarine
2 tablespoons dry white wine
½ teaspoon cornstarch
⅛ teaspoon salt
Dash pepper
8 seedless green grapes, halved
Hot cooked rice

Halve chicken livers. In small skillet cook livers and onion in butter or margarine about 5 minutes or till livers are just barely pink inside. Combine wine, cornstarch, salt, and pepper; add to chicken livers. Cook and stir till thickened and bubbly. Stir in halved green grapes. Serve over rice. Makes 1 serving.

Microwave cooking directions: Halve chicken livers; set aside. In small shallow nonmetal baking dish, combine onion and butter or margarine. Cook in countertop microwave oven on high power about 1 minute or till tender. Add livers to onion mixture, stirring to coat well.

Combine wine, cornstarch, salt, and pepper. Pour wine mixture over liver and onion mixture. Micro-cook, covered with waxed paper, for 1½ to 2 minutes or till livers are just pink inside, stirring twice. Stir in grapes. Serve liver mixture over rice.

Broiled Apple-Stuffed Chicken

1 2- to 2½-pound broiler-fryer chicken, halved lengthwise
2 tablespoons butter *or* margarine, melted
1 cup chopped apple
¼ cup chopped onion
¼ cup chopped celery
¼ cup butter *or* margarine
2 cups herb-seasoned croutons
⅓ cup water
¼ teaspoon salt
Dash pepper

Preheat broiler. Break wing, hip, and drumstick joints of chicken so bird will remain flat during broiling. Twist wing tips under back. Place chicken, skin side up, in broiler pan.* Brush with *half* of the melted butter or margarine; sprinkle with a little salt and pepper. Broil 5 to 6 inches from heat about 20 minutes or till lightly browned. Turn and brush cavity side with the remaining melted butter or margarine; sprinkle with a little salt and pepper. Broil 15 to 20 minutes or till tender.

Meanwhile, cook apple, onion, and celery in ¼ cup butter or margarine till tender. Toss with croutons, water, ¼ teaspoon salt, and dash pepper. Season to taste with additional salt, if desired. Heap cavity of each chicken half with apple mixture. Cover the legs with foil to prevent excess browning. Broil about 5 minutes longer. Garnish with parsley and apple slices, if desired. Makes 2 servings. (Adaptable for one.)†

To decide whether or not to use a broiler rack, place chicken on an unheated rack in the broiler pan, then place under broiler. If there aren't 5 to 6 inches between the chicken and the heat, remove the rack and place chicken directly in the broiler pan.

†See page 3 for directions.

Chicken Pot Pies

2 tablespoons chopped onion
2 tablespoons butter *or*
  margarine
2 tablespoons all-purpose
  flour
1 teaspoon instant chicken
  bouillon granules
¼ teaspoon salt
⅛ teaspoon ground sage
  Dash pepper
⅔ cup milk
½ cup water
1 cup cubed cooked chicken *or*
  turkey
½ cup frozen mixed vegetables,
  cooked and drained
1 tablespoon snipped parsley
1 package (6) refrigerated
  biscuits

Cook onion in butter or margarine till tender but not brown. Blend in flour, chicken bouillon granules, salt, sage, and pepper. Add milk and water. Cook and stir till thickened and bubbly. Stir in chicken or turkey, vegetables, and parsley; heat till bubbly. Pour into 2 individual casseroles.

Quarter 2 of the biscuits; set aside remaining biscuits. In each casserole place half of the biscuit pieces atop *hot* filling. Place casseroles on a baking sheet. Arrange remaining biscuits on baking sheet alongside casseroles. Bake in 400° oven for 10 to 12 minutes or till biscuits are lightly browned. Serve extra biscuits with pies or save for another meal. Makes 2 servings. (Adaptable for one.)†

Stir-Fried Sweet and Sour Chicken

1 whole medium chicken
  breast, skinned, split, and
  boned
1 small sweet red *or* green
  pepper
1 8¼-ounce can pineapple
  chunks
2 teaspoons cornstarch
2 tablespoons soy sauce
2 tablespoons dry sherry
1 tablespoon honey
1 tablespoon vinegar
  Dash pepper
1 tablespoon cooking oil
  Hot cooked rice

Cut chicken into 1-inch pieces. Cut red or green pepper into ¾-inch squares. Drain pineapple, reserving juice; set pineapple aside. In small bowl blend reserved pineapple juice and cornstarch; stir in soy sauce, sherry, honey, vinegar, and pepper. Set mixture aside.

Preheat a large skillet or wok over high heat; add cooking oil. Add red or green pepper; cook and stir 2 minutes. Remove from skillet. (Add more cooking oil, if necessary.) Add chicken; cook and stir 2 minutes. Stir soy mixture; blend into chicken. Cook and stir till thickened and bubbly. Add red or green pepper and pineapple; cover and cook 1 minute. Serve over hot cooked rice. Makes 2 servings. (Adaptable for one.)†

Creamy Chicken Tarragon

1 whole medium chicken
  breast, skinned, split, and
  boned
2 tablespoons all-purpose
  flour
¼ teaspoon salt
¼ teaspoon dried tarragon,
  crushed
¼ teaspoon finely shredded
  lemon peel
1 tablespoon cooking oil
⅓ cup water
⅓ cup milk
½ teaspoon instant chicken
  bouillon granules
1 teaspoon lemon juice
  Hot cooked parslied rice

Place each piece of chicken between 2 pieces clear plastic wrap. Pound with meat mallet to flatten slightly. Remove wrap. Cut chicken into 1½-inch pieces. In plastic bag combine flour, salt, tarragon, and lemon peel. Shake chicken pieces in flour mixture to coat evenly. Reserve the remaining flour mixture.

In an 8-inch skillet cook chicken in hot oil for 4 to 5 minutes or till tender and browned. Remove from skillet. Blend the remaining flour mixture into pan drippings. Add water, milk, and bouillon granules. Cook and stir till thickened and bubbly. Stir in lemon juice. Add chicken and cook till heated through. Spoon over hot parslied rice. Makes 2 servings. (Adaptable for one.)†

†See page 3 for directions.

When you need a quick supper dish, turn to Chicken Pot Pies. Each casserole is full of mixed vegetables and chicken topped with flaky biscuits.

Chicken Pilaf

4 chicken drumsticks *or* thighs
  or 2 whole small chicken
  breasts, split
1 tablespoon butter *or*
  margarine
⅓ cup long grain rice
¼ cup chopped onion
⅔ cup water
2 tablespoons raisins
1 tablespoon snipped parsley
1 teaspoon instant chicken
  bouillon granules
1 teaspoon finely shredded
  orange peel
¼ teaspoon salt
  Parsley sprigs (optional)

In skillet brown chicken pieces in butter or margarine. Sprinkle lightly with a little salt and pepper; remove chicken from skillet. Cook rice and onion in skillet drippings, stirring constantly, till rice is light golden brown. Stir in water, raisins, snipped parsley, chicken bouillon granules, shredded orange peel, and salt. Bring rice mixture to boiling.

Turn into a 1-quart casserole. Top with browned chicken pieces. Cover and bake in 375° oven for 45 to 50 minutes or till chicken and rice are tender. Garnish with parsley sprigs, if desired. Makes 2 servings.

Turkey Drumstick Dinner

½ cup finely chopped onion
½ cup finely chopped carrot
½ cup finely chopped celery
3 tablespoons catsup
½ teaspoon salt
¼ teaspoon paprika
  Dash pepper
1 turkey drumstick (1½ to 2
  pounds)
4 teaspoons all-purpose flour
¼ cup water
3 tablespoons dry white wine
½ teaspoon dried oregano,
  crushed
¼ teaspoon instant chicken
  bouillon granules
1 bay leaf, crumbled
2 tablespoons cold water

In mixing bowl combine onion, carrot, celery, catsup, salt, paprika, and pepper; pat vegetable mixture over turkey drumstick. Place *1 teaspoon* of the flour in an oven roasting bag; shake to coat inside. Place bag in 10×6×2-inch baking dish. Carefully transfer drumstick to bag. Combine ¼ cup water, wine, oregano, bouillon granules, and bay leaf; pour into bag. Close bag; fasten with twist tie. Cut slits in top of bag. Bake in 350° oven about 1½ hours or till tender.

Remove drumstick to platter; keep warm. Pour liquid and vegetables into a saucepan; boil vigorously till liquid is reduced to 1 cup. Blend 2 tablespoons cold water into the remaining *3 teaspoons* flour; stir into liquid in pan. Cook and stir till mixture is thickened and bubbly. Slice turkey; pass gravy with meat. Makes 2 servings.

Oven Chicken with Vegetables

2 chicken drumsticks *or* thighs
2 tablespoons butter *or*
  margarine, melted
2 tablespoons fine dry bread
  crumbs
1 tablespoon grated parmesan
  cheese
⅛ teaspoon dried oregano,
  crushed
1 or 2 carrots
1 medium potato, peeled and
  halved lengthwise
  Dried dillweed

Brush chicken pieces with some of the melted butter or margarine, then roll in mixture of bread crumbs, parmesan cheese, and oregano to coat. Place chicken, skin side up, in 8×8×2-inch baking pan. Halve carrots crosswise, then lengthwise. Arrange cut-up carrots and potato around chicken in pan. Sprinkle chicken and vegetables generously with salt and pepper. Bake in 375° oven for 30 minutes.

Brush vegetables with the remaining melted butter; bake about 25 minutes longer or till chicken and vegetables are tender. Sprinkle potato with dillweed. Makes 1 serving.

 Beef

Steak-Lobster Dinner
(pictured on the cover)

1 5-ounce frozen lobster tail
2 6-ounce beef tenderloin *or* top loin steaks
1 tablespoon butter *or* margarine
1 tablespoon sliced green onion
1 tablespoon all-purpose flour
⅛ teaspoon salt
Dash white pepper
½ cup milk
½ cup shredded *process* Swiss cheese (2 ounces)
1 2½-ounce jar sliced mushrooms, drained
2 tablespoons dry white wine

Drop frozen lobster tail into enough boiling salted water to cover. Bring to boiling. Reduce heat and simmer for 5 to 6 minutes; drain. Snip along each side of the thin undershell. Remove undershell to expose the meat. Grasp tail with one hand and insert index finger of the other hand between shell and meat. Pull shell away from meat, separating meat and shell. Cut meat into pieces. Set aside.

Slash fat edge of top loin steaks at 1-inch intervals. Place tenderloin or top loin steaks on unheated rack in broiler pan. Broil 3 inches from heat till desired doneness, turning once (allow about 12 minutes total for medium-rare). Season with a little salt and pepper.

Meanwhile, in saucepan melt butter or margarine; add green onion and cook till tender. Blend in flour, salt, and white pepper. Add milk. Cook and stir till thickened and bubbly. Stir in cheese, mushrooms, wine, and lobster. Cook and stir till lobster is heated through.

Place steaks on plates; spoon lobster mixture over each steak. Top with snipped parsley, if desired. Makes 2 servings.

Baked Veal Parmesan

3 tablespoons fine dry bread crumbs
3 tablespoons grated parmesan cheese
Dash pepper
1 beaten egg
1 teaspoon water
2 veal cutlets, cut ¼ inch thick (about ½ pound)
¼ cup catsup *or* tomato sauce
2 teaspoons water
¼ teaspoon dried oregano, crushed
Dash onion salt
Dash pepper
2 ounces mozzarella cheese, thinly sliced

Combine crumbs, parmesan cheese, and dash pepper. Combine egg and 1 teaspoon water. Dip veal in egg mixture; coat with crumb mixture. Arrange veal in 10×6×2-inch baking dish. Bake in 400° oven for 20 minutes. Turn meat; bake about 15 minutes more or till nearly tender.

Meanwhile, combine catsup or tomato sauce, 2 teaspoons water, oregano, onion salt, and dash pepper. Spoon catsup mixture over meat in baking dish; bake for 5 minutes. Top with mozzarella cheese slices. Bake 1 to 2 minutes more or till cheese melts. Makes 2 servings. (Adaptable for one.)†

†See page 3 for directions.

Beef sirloin three-way dinners

Divide one 2½-pound beef sirloin steak, cut 1½ inches thick, into 2 pieces as follows:

Remove the large center muscle for **Lemon Barbecued Steak**. Cut out the bone and trim off fat. (This muscle should weigh about 1¾ pounds before trimming, about 1¼ pounds after trimming.) Cut the remaining steak into 1½×1-inch pieces for **Beef Kabobs Burgundy**. (This portion of steak should weigh about ¾ pound.)

To prepare **Sirloin Salad Supreme**, use ½ pound or more leftover meat from **Lemon Barbecued Steak**.

Storing meat: A fresh piece of steak may be stored in the refrigerator for 2 to 4 days. Cooked meat may be refrigerated for 4 to 5 days. For longer storage, wrap the meat tightly in moisture-vapor-proof wrap and freeze.

Sirloin Salad Supreme

Lemon Barbecued Steak

Lemon Barbecued Steak

1¼ pounds boneless beef
    sirloin steak
½ teaspoon finely shredded
    lemon peel
⅓ cup lemon juice
2 tablespoons cooking oil
1 green onion, sliced
¾ teaspoon salt
½ teaspoon prepared mustard
½ teaspoon worcestershire
    sauce
⅛ teaspoon pepper

Place meat in plastic bag; set in
shallow pan. For marinade
combine remaining ingredients;
pour over meat. Close bag;
marinate 2 to 4 hours in refrigerator; turn meat occasionally. Drain; reserve marinade.

Place meat on grill over
medium-hot coals. Grill till desired doneness, turning once (allow 20 to 25 minutes total for
medium-rare). Brush meat occasionally with reserved marinade. Store about ½ pound
cooked steak to use in *Sirloin
Salad Supreme.* Serves 2.

Beef Kabobs Burgundy

¾ pound beef sirloin steak, cut
    into 1½×1-inch pieces
½ cup burgundy
2 tablespoons cooking oil
1 tablespoon snipped candied
    ginger
1 tablespoon light molasses
¼ teaspoon salt
    Dash garlic powder
    Dash pepper

Place meat in plastic bag; set in
shallow pan. For marinade combine the remaining ingredients;
pour over meat. Close bag;
marinate for 2 to 4 hours or overnight in the refrigerator, turning
meat occasionally. Drain meat,
reserving marinade.

Thread meat on 2 skewers.
Grill over *medium-hot* coals till
desired doneness (allow 18 to 20
minutes total for medium-rare).
Turn and brush often with reserved marinade. (If desired,
grill mushrooms, zucchini, and
cherry tomatoes on separate
skewers about 10 minutes or till
tender.) Makes 2 servings.

Sirloin Salad Supreme

½ pound cooked *Lemon
    Barbecued Steak*
    Lettuce leaves
4 cups torn mixed salad
    greens
1 medium tomato, cut into thin
    wedges
1 avocado, seeded, peeled,
    and sliced
    Whole black peppercorns
2 ounces blue cheese,
    crumbled (½ cup)
¼ cup mayonnaise
¼ teaspoon worcestershire
    sauce
½ cup buttermilk

Using leftover meat from *Lemon
Barbecued Steak,* thinly slice
meat (should measure about 1½
cups). Sprinkle with a little salt
and pepper. Line a salad bowl
with lettuce leaves. Arrange torn
mixed greens, tomato, avocado,
and meat in bowl. Grind pepper
over salad. Chill. For dressing
have cheese at room tem-
perature. Combine cheese, mayonnaise, and worcestershire.
Gradually beat in buttermilk.
Serve with salad. Makes 2 servings (1 cup dressing).

Beef Kabobs Burgundy

Beef Short Rib Stew

10 to 12 ounces beef short ribs
½ of an envelope *regular*
    vegetable soup mix
¼ cup all-purpose flour
½ teaspoon paprika
¼ teaspoon salt
    Dash pepper
 1 medium potato, peeled and
    halved
 1 medium carrot, halved
    lengthwise
 1 small stalk celery, cut up
 1 slice onion
¼ cup dry sherry

Cut ribs into serving-size pieces; trim off excess fat. In an oven roasting bag combine ribs, soup mix, flour, paprika, salt, and pepper. Shake well. Add vegetables, sherry, and 1 cup *water*. Close bag; fasten with twist tie. Place in shallow baking pan. Cut slits in top of bag. Bake in 400° oven about 1½ hours or till meat is tender. Makes 1 serving.

Prepare a small roast when you want to enjoy roast beef without having more leftovers than you can readily use.

To roast a 4-pound beef rib roast, sprinkle with salt and pepper. Place, fat side up, on rack in shallow roasting pan. Insert a meat thermometer into center of meat. Roast in 325° oven 1¾ to 2 hours for rare (or till thermometer registers 140°), 2¼ to 2½ hours for medium (160°), or 2½ to 3 hours for well-done (170°). Let stand 15 minutes for easier carving.

The slow-and-easy simmering needed to cook Short Ribs with Limas in a tangy barbecue-flavored sauce is well worth the wait.

Short Ribs with Limas

 1 pound beef short ribs, cut
    into serving-size pieces
 1 small onion, sliced
 1 bay leaf
½ cup water
 3 tablespoons brown sugar
 2 tablespoons vinegar
½ teaspoon dry mustard
 1 tablespoon cold water
 2 teaspoons cornstarch
 1 16-ounce can butter beans*,
    drained

Trim excess fat from short ribs. Place ribs in *unheated* 3-quart saucepan; brown meat on all sides over medium-high heat. Sprinkle with a little salt and pepper. Add onion, bay leaf, ½ cup water, brown sugar, vinegar, and mustard. Cover and simmer for 1¾ to 2 hours or till ribs are tender.

Remove ribs. Skim excess fat from meat juices. Blend 1 tablespoon water and cornstarch; stir into meat juices. Cook and stir till thickened and bubbly. Add short ribs and butter beans. Cover and simmer about 10 minutes longer. Turn into serving dish. Makes 2 servings.

Butter beans might also be labeled cooked dry lima beans.

Pot Roast Dinner

¾ pound boneless beef chuck
    pot roast
1 tablespoon cooking oil
½ teaspoon salt
⅛ teaspoon pepper
1 cup water
1 teaspoon instant beef
    bouillon granules
¼ teaspoon worcestershire
    sauce
1 bay leaf
1 clove garlic, minced
2 medium carrots, halved
    crosswise
2 medium potatoes, peeled
    and quartered
1 small onion, quartered
1 small green pepper,
    quartered
1 tablespoon cornstarch
1 tablespoon cold water
    Several drops Kitchen
    Bouquet (optional)
1 tablespoon snipped parsley

In heavy skillet slowly brown meat on both sides in hot oil. Season with salt and pepper. Add 1 cup water, bouillon granules, worcestershire, bay leaf, and garlic; cover and simmer for 1 hour. Add carrots, potatoes, and onion; sprinkle lightly with salt. Simmer for 40 minutes. Add green pepper; simmer about 5 minutes longer or till meat is tender. Remove meat and vegetables to warm serving platter.

Pour pan juices into measuring cup; skim off fat. Add enough water to pan juices to make 1 cup liquid. Return to skillet. Blend cornstarch and 1 tablespoon water; stir into pan juices. Add Kitchen Bouquet, if desired. Cook and stir till thickened and bubbly. Spoon some gravy over meat and vegetables; pass remaining gravy. Garnish with parsley. Makes 2 servings.

Steak Bertrand

1 beef cubed steak
3 tablespoons water
1 tablespoon dry red wine
1 teaspoon snipped parsley
    Dash garlic powder
2 teaspoons butter or
    margarine
½ teaspoon cornstarch
¼ cup sliced fresh mushrooms
1 triangle Swiss cheese

Place steak in plastic bag; set in shallow bowl. Add water, wine, parsley, and garlic powder. Close bag. Marinate 15 minutes at room temperature or 1 hour in refrigerator, turning meat once. Drain meat, reserving wine mixture. Pat meat dry with paper toweling; sprinkle with a little salt and pepper.

In small skillet melt butter or margarine over medium-high heat. Cook meat in butter for 2 minutes. Turn and cook about 2 minutes more. Blend cornstarch and wine mixture; stir into pan drippings. Add sliced fresh mushrooms; bring to boiling. Top meat with Swiss cheese. Cover and heat about 1 minute or till cheese melts. Serve wine-mushroom mixture with meat. Makes 1 serving.

Bavarian Supper

2 beef cubed steaks
1 tablespoon cooking oil
2 tablespoons chopped onion
1 ¾-ounce envelope mushroom
    gravy mix
1 tablespoon vinegar
2 teaspoons brown sugar
½ teaspoon caraway seed
2 cups coarsely shredded
    cabbage
1 medium potato, peeled and
    cubed

Quickly brown steaks in hot oil. Add onion; cook about 3 minutes or till almost tender. Combine gravy mix, vinegar, brown sugar, caraway, and 1 cup water; pour over steaks. Cover and simmer for 15 minutes.

Meanwhile, in covered pan cook cabbage and potato in boiling salted water for 5 to 7 minutes or till tender; drain. Spoon onto serving platter; arrange steaks atop vegetables. Serve with gravy. Makes 2 servings.

Reuben Casserole

1 8-ounce can sauerkraut
⅛ teaspoon caraway seed
1 small tomato, cut into thin
    wedges
2 tablespoons thousand island
    salad dressing
1 3- or 4-ounce package thinly
    sliced corned beef, cut up
¼ cup shredded Swiss cheese
½ cup soft rye bread crumbs
2 teaspoons butter, melted

Drain sauerkraut; place in 3-cup baking dish. Sprinkle with caraway; top with tomato, salad dressing, and beef. Top with cheese. Toss bread crumbs with butter; sprinkle over casserole. Bake in 375° oven 25 to 30 minutes or till heated through. Makes 2 servings.

Steak and Shrimp Creole

½ pound beef round steak, cut ¾ inch thick
2 tablespoons cooking oil
2 tablespoons thinly sliced green onion
2 tablespoons coarsely chopped green pepper
2 tablespoons coarsely chopped celery
1 8-ounce can tomato sauce
¼ cup water
⅛ teaspoon salt
  Dash pepper
  Dash garlic powder
  Few drops bottled hot pepper sauce
1 cup frozen shelled tiny shrimp
  Hot cooked rice

Cut meat into 2 serving-size pieces. In 8-inch skillet brown meat in hot oil. Remove meat from skillet. In skillet drippings cook onion, green pepper, and celery till tender but not brown. Stir in tomato sauce, water, salt, pepper, garlic powder, and hot pepper sauce.

Bring to boiling. Reduce heat; add the browned meat. Cover and simmer for 40 to 45 minutes or till tender. Add shrimp and simmer about 5 minutes more or till shrimp is cooked. Serve over rice. Makes 2 servings.

Beef in Olive-Tomato Sauce

½ pound beef top round steak *or* flank steak
1 tablespoon cooking oil
2 tablespoons chopped onion
1 clove garlic, minced
1 teaspoon instant beef bouillon granules
½ teaspoon sugar
½ cup dairy sour cream
1 tablespoon all-purpose flour
1 8-ounce can tomatoes, cut up
1 2-ounce can mushroom stems and pieces, drained
¼ cup sliced pitted ripe olives
2 tablespoons dry white wine
  Hot cooked noodles

Score flank steak on both sides. Partially freeze round or flank steak; cut into 2×¼-inch strips. Brown quickly in hot oil; remove from skillet. Add onion and garlic; cook till tender. Return meat to skillet. Stir in bouillon granules, sugar, ¼ teaspoon *salt*, and dash *pepper*. Combine sour cream and flour; add sour cream mixture, tomatoes, mushrooms, olives, and wine to skillet. Cook and stir till thick. Serve over noodles. Makes 2 servings.

Microwave cooking directions: Cut steak into strips as above. Allow steak to thaw completely. In 1-quart nonmetal casserole combine meat, oil, onion, and garlic. Cook, covered with waxed paper, in countertop microwave oven on high power for 2½ minutes; stir once. Stir in bouillon granules, sugar, ¼ teaspoon *salt,* and dash *pepper.* Stir together sour cream and flour. Add sour cream mixture, tomatoes, mushrooms, olives, and wine to casserole. Micro-cook, covered, about 4 minutes, stirring 3 times. Serve as above.

Garden Swiss Steak

½ pound beef round steak, cut ¾ inch thick
1 tablespoon all-purpose flour
½ teaspoon salt
  Dash pepper
¼ cup chopped onion
1 tablespoon cooking oil
1 cup water
½ teaspoon instant beef bouillon granules
6 tiny whole carrots *or* 2 medium carrots, cut into 1-inch pieces
1 small zucchini, sliced (1 cup)
¼ teaspoon dried dillweed
1 small tomato, peeled, cored, and cut into wedges

Cut meat into 2 serving-size pieces. Combine flour, salt, and pepper; pound thoroughly into meat, using meat mallet. In 8-inch skillet brown meat and onion in hot oil. Remove from heat.

Add water and beef bouillon granules. Return to heat and simmer, covered, for 35 minutes. Add carrots; cover and simmer for 12 minutes. Add zucchini and dillweed; sprinkle with additional salt and pepper. Continue cooking about 5 minutes longer or till meat and vegetables are tender. Add tomato wedges to meat mixture and heat through. Makes 2 servings.

Feature Garden Swiss Steak for an eye-catching entrée. Fresh summer vegetables and a generous sprinkling of dill accent the round steak.

Sweet and Sour Liver Skewers

½ of an 8-ounce can (2)
     pineapple slices
2 tablespoons water
2 tablespoons soy sauce
1 tablespoon dry sherry
1 tablespoon vinegar
2 teaspoons cornstarch
½ pound beef liver, cut into
     1½-inch-wide strips
½ small green pepper, cut into
     1-inch squares

Drain off 2 tablespoons of syrup from the pineapple; set aside. Quarter the 2 pineapple slices; set aside. In saucepan combine the reserved 2 tablespoons pineapple syrup, water, soy sauce, sherry, vinegar, and cornstarch; cook and stir till mixture is thickened and bubbly.

On two 10-inch skewers alternately thread liver, accordion-style, with green pepper and pineapple pieces. Place skewers on unheated rack in broiler pan. Broil 3 inches from heat about 8 minutes or till meat is done, turning once. Brush occasionally with soy sauce mixture. (If you don't have skewers, you may broil the liver, green pepper, and pineapple in a single layer on the broiler rack.) Makes 2 servings. (Adaptable for one.)†

Sautéed Liver and Vegetables

1 small green pepper, cut into
     rings
1 small onion, sliced
1 tablespoon cooking oil *or*
     shortening
2 slices beef liver, cut ⅜ inch
     thick (about ½ pound)
1 teaspoon water
1 teaspoon lemon juice
½ teaspoon worcestershire
     sauce
¼ teaspoon dried oregano,
     crushed

Halve large green pepper rings. In an 8-inch skillet cook green pepper and onion in hot oil or shortening till tender but not brown. Remove from skillet.

Add liver slices to skillet; sprinkle with a little salt and pepper. Cook for 3 minutes over medium heat; turn liver. Return green pepper and onion to skillet. Cook about 3 minutes more or till liver is done. Remove skillet from heat.

Transfer liver, green pepper, and onion to serving platter. Blend water, lemon juice, worcestershire sauce, and oregano into pan drippings; pour over liver. Makes 2 servings. (Adaptable for one.)†

Saucy Meatballs

1 beaten egg
1 slice white bread, torn up
1 tablespoon catsup
¼ teaspoon salt
     Dash pepper
½ pound ground beef
1 7½-ounce can semi-
     condensed cream of
     mushroom with wine soup
½ of an 8-ounce can (½ cup)
     tomato sauce
2 tablespoons finely chopped
     onion
2 tablespoons finely chopped
     green pepper
     Hot cooked rice *or* noodles

In a small mixing bowl combine beaten egg, bread, catsup, salt, and pepper. Add ground beef; mix well. Shape mixture into 1-inch meatballs. Set aside.

In skillet combine soup and tomato sauce. Bring to boiling, stirring occasionally. Add meatballs, onion, and green pepper. Cover and simmer about 20 minutes or till meatballs are cooked, stirring occasionally. Serve over rice or noodles. Makes 2 servings.

Microwave cooking directions: Prepare the meatballs as above. Arrange in 10×6×2-inch nonmetal baking dish. Cook, covered with waxed paper, in countertop microwave oven on high power for 5 minutes, rearranging meatballs once. Drain off fat.

In bowl combine soup, tomato sauce, onion, and green pepper; pour atop meatballs, stirring to rearrange. Micro-cook, covered, for 5 to 6 minutes, stirring once. Serve as above.

Prepare intriguing Scotch Meat Loaves *by shaping the meat mixture around hard-cooked eggs, adding a chili sauce topping, and baking.*

Scotch Meat Loaves

1 beaten egg
¼ cup soft bread crumbs
2 tablespoons finely chopped celery
2 tablespoons finely chopped onion
¼ teaspoon salt
⅛ teaspoon ground sage
   Dash garlic powder
½ pound lean ground beef
2 hard-cooked eggs
¼ cup chili sauce
1 tablespoon snipped parsley
1 tablespoon water
⅛ teaspoon dried oregano, crushed
1 slice sharp American cheese, shredded *or* sliced

In mixing bowl combine beaten egg, bread crumbs, celery, onion, salt, sage, and garlic powder. Add ground beef; mix well. Shape half of the meat mixture around each hard-cooked egg, completely enclosing egg. Arrange meat loaves in a 6½×6½×2-inch baking dish.

Combine chili sauce, parsley, water, and oregano; pour over meat loaves. Bake in 350° oven for 45 minutes. Spoon chili sauce mixture over loaves; top each with some cheese. Return to oven and heat till cheese melts. Makes 2 servings.

Tangy Meat Loaf

1 beaten egg
2 tablespoons quick-cooking rolled oats
2 tablespoons sliced pimiento-stuffed olives
2 tablespoons grated parmesan cheese
1 tablespoon chopped onion
¼ teaspoon salt
⅛ teaspoon pepper
½ pound ground beef
¼ cup catsup
1 tablespoon snipped parsley
1 tablespoon water

In mixing bowl combine egg, rolled oats, olives, cheese, onion, salt, and pepper. Add ground beef; mix well. Pat into a 6×3×2-inch loaf pan. In small bowl combine catsup, parsley, and water; pour over meat mixture. Bake in 350° oven about 50 minutes. Makes 2 servings.

Microwave cooking directions: Prepare meat mixture as above. In a 9-inch nonmetal pie plate shape mixture into a 1-inch-thick round loaf. Cook, covered with waxed paper, in countertop microwave oven on high power for 5 minutes; drain off fat.

Combine catsup, parsley, and water; pour mixture over meat loaf. Micro-cook, uncovered, about 2 minutes more. Let stand 2 minutes before serving.

†See page 3 for directions.

Burgers Stroganoff

1 beaten egg
¼ cup soft bread crumbs
½ teaspoon dried basil, crushed
¼ teaspoon salt
½ pound lean ground beef
1 tablespoon butter *or* margarine
1 cup sliced fresh mushrooms
2 tablespoons sliced green onion
½ cup dairy sour cream
½ teaspoon all-purpose flour
2 tablespoons dry white wine
1 teaspoon snipped parsley
¼ teaspoon salt
   Dash pepper
   Hot cooked noodles
   Snipped parsley (optional)

In mixing bowl combine egg, bread crumbs, basil, and ¼ teaspoon salt. Add ground beef and mix well. Shape into two 1½-inch-thick patties. Cook over medium-high heat till desired doneness, turning once (allow 10 to 12 minutes total for medium).

Meanwhile, for sauce melt butter or margarine in saucepan; add mushrooms and onion. Cook about 3 minutes or till tender, stirring occasionally. Combine sour cream and flour; stir in wine, 1 teaspoon snipped parsley, ¼ teaspoon salt, and pepper. Add to mushroom mixture. Cook and stir till thickened and bubbly.

Place meat patties atop hot cooked noodles; spoon sauce over meat. Sprinkle with additional snipped parsley, if desired. Makes 2 servings.

Sproutburger

¼ cup soft bread crumbs
3 tablespoons fresh *or* canned bean sprouts
1 tablespoon chopped onion
1 tablespoon catsup
2 teaspoons soy sauce
⅛ teaspoon dry mustard
¼ pound ground beef
2 tablespoons wheat germ
2 teaspoons cooking oil
1 hamburger bun, split and toasted

Mix bread, sprouts, onion, catsup, soy, mustard, and dash *pepper.* Add meat; mix well. Shape into one ¾-inch-thick patty; coat with wheat germ. Fry in hot oil over medium heat till desired doneness; turn once (allow about 10 minutes total for medium). Serve in bun. Makes 1 serving.

Beefed-Up Peppers

2 large green peppers
½ pound ground beef
2 tablespoons chopped onion
½ of an 8¾-ounce can whole kernel corn, drained
¼ cup shredded cheddar cheese
¼ cup chili sauce
½ teaspoon chili powder
½ teaspoon worcestershire sauce
¼ cup crushed taco chips

Cut off tops of peppers; chop and set aside. Remove seeds and membranes from pepper cups. Precook in boiling salted water 5 minutes; drain. Cook chopped pepper, meat, and onion till meat is browned; drain fat. Stir in corn, cheese, chili sauce, chili powder, worcestershire, and ¼ teaspoon *salt.* Stuff peppers; place upright in 1- or 1½-quart casserole. Top with chips. Bake in 350° oven 40 to 45 minutes. Makes 2 servings. (Adaptable for one.)†

Chili for Two

½ pound ground beef
¼ cup chopped green pepper
¼ cup chopped onion
1 clove garlic, minced
1 8-ounce can tomatoes, cut up
1 8-ounce can tomato sauce
1 8-ounce can red kidney
   beans
1 to 1½ teaspoons chili
   powder
¼ teaspoon salt
¼ teaspoon dried basil,
   crushed
⅛ teaspoon pepper
   Hot cooked rice *or* corn
   bread squares (optional)

In skillet cook ground beef, green pepper, onion, and garlic till meat is browned. Drain off excess fat. Stir in tomatoes, tomato sauce, *undrained* kidney beans, chili powder, salt, basil, and pepper. Bring to boiling; reduce heat. Cover and simmer about 20 minutes. Serve in bowls. Or, spoon over hot cooked rice or serve with cornbread squares, if desired. Makes 2 servings.

Microwave cooking directions:
In a 1-quart nonmetal casserole crumble ground beef. Add green pepper, onion, and garlic. Cook, covered with waxed paper, in countertop microwave oven on high power about 4 minutes or till meat is browned. Stir several times to break up meat. Drain off excess fat.

Stir in tomatoes, tomato sauce, *undrained* kidney beans, chili powder, salt, basil, and pepper. Micro-cook, covered, about 8 minutes, stirring mixture twice. Serve as above.

Herbed Spaghetti Sauce

½ pound ground beef
¼ cup finely chopped onion
¼ cup finely chopped green
   pepper
1 clove garlic, minced
1 10¾-ounce can condensed
   tomato soup
1 8-ounce can tomato sauce
1 2-ounce can mushroom
   stems and pieces, drained
1 bay leaf
¼ teaspoon salt
¼ teaspoon dried oregano,
   crushed
¼ teaspoon dried basil,
   crushed
⅛ teaspoon dried rosemary,
   crushed
⅛ teaspoon dried thyme,
   crushed
   Dash pepper
   Hot cooked spaghetti
   Grated parmesan cheese

In 8-inch skillet cook ground beef, onion, green pepper, and garlic till meat is browned. Drain off excess fat.

Stir in soup and tomato sauce. Stir in mushrooms, bay leaf, salt, oregano, basil, rosemary, thyme, and pepper. Bring to boiling; reduce heat. Cover and simmer about 30 minutes, stirring occasionally. Discard bay leaf. Serve over hot cooked spaghetti; pass parmesan cheese. Makes 3 cups sauce.

Beef and Rice Espagnole

½ pound ground beef
¼ cup chopped onion
1 8-ounce can tomato sauce
¼ cup quick-cooking rice*
2 tablespoons chopped pitted
   ripe olives
2 tablespoons rinsed, seeded,
   chopped canned green
   chili peppers
¼ teaspoon garlic salt
⅛ teaspoon pepper
   Few drops bottled hot
   pepper sauce
½ cup American cheese cut
   into ½-inch cubes
   (2 ounces)

In skillet cook meat and onion till meat is browned and onion is tender; drain off fat. Combine tomato sauce, rice, olives, chilies, garlic salt, pepper, hot pepper sauce, and ¼ cup *water*. Stir into meat mixture; bring to boiling.

Turn into a 3-cup casserole. Cover and bake in 350° oven about 20 minutes or till rice is tender. Add cheese cubes, stirring just till cubes are distributed. Let stand 1 to 2 minutes before serving. Makes 2 servings.

Microwave cooking directions:
In a 3-cup nonmetal casserole crumble meat. Add onion. Cook, covered with waxed paper, in countertop microwave oven on high power for 3 to 4 minutes or till meat is browned and onion is tender. Stir once or twice to break up meat. Drain off fat.

Combine tomato sauce, rice*, olives, chilies, garlic salt, pepper, pepper sauce, and 2 tablespoons *water*. Stir into meat mixture. Micro-cook, covered, for 7 to 8 minutes or till rice is tender, stirring after 4 minutes. Add cheese; stir just till distributed. Let stand 1 to 2 minutes before serving.

Use Minute Rice when preparing casserole in a microwave oven.

†See page 3 for directions.

Pork & Ham

Pennsylvania Dutch Pork Steaks *is an easy skillet entrée that nestles applesauce-topped pork on a bed of sauerkraut and caraway.*

Pennsylvania Dutch Pork Steaks

2 pork shoulder steaks, cut ½ inch thick (about 1 pound)
1 tablespoon shortening *or* cooking oil
1 8-ounce can sauerkraut
½ teaspoon caraway seed
½ cup applesauce
2 tablespoons finely chopped onion
Parsley sprigs (optional)

In medium skillet slowly brown steaks on both sides in hot shortening or oil. Remove from skillet; drain off excess fat. Drain sauerkraut, reserving 2 tablespoons liquid. Snip sauerkraut. In same skillet combine sauerkraut, the reserved 2 tablespoons liquid, and caraway seed. Place steaks atop sauerkraut mixture; sprinkle with a little salt and pepper. Cover and simmer about 30 minutes or till pork steaks are nearly tender.

Combine applesauce and chopped onion; spoon atop steaks. Cover and cook about 5 minutes more or till meat is tender and applesauce is heated through. Garnish with parsley, if desired. Makes 2 servings.

Mushroom-Stuffed Pork Chops

2 pork loin rib chops, cut 1 to 1¼ inches thick (about 1¼ pounds)
1 2-ounce can chopped mushrooms, drained
1 tablespoon snipped parsley
1 tablespoon finely chopped onion
¼ teaspoon salt
Dash pepper
1 slice Swiss cheese, torn up (1 ounce)
1 slightly beaten egg
¼ cup fine dry bread crumbs
1 tablespoon cooking oil
⅓ cup water
¼ cup dry white wine
1 tablespoon cornstarch
1 tablespoon cold water

Trim excess fat from chops; sprinkle meat with a little salt and pepper. Cut pocket in fat side of each chop. Combine mushrooms, parsley, onion, salt, and pepper. Place cheese in pockets of chops; stuff with mushroom mixture. Reserve any leftover mushroom mixture for the sauce.

Dip chops in beaten egg, then in bread crumbs. In an 8-inch skillet slowly brown chops in hot oil. Add the ⅓ cup water and the wine. Cover and simmer about 1 hour or till meat is tender. Transfer meat to serving platter; keep warm.

For sauce blend the cornstarch and 1 tablespoon cold water; stir into wine mixture. Cook and stir till thickened and bubbly. Stir in any reserved mushroom mixture; heat through. Serve over meat. Makes 2 servings.

Hawaiian Smoked Pork Chops

1 8-ounce can pineapple slices
¼ cup chopped green pepper
2 tablespoons apricot preserves
½ teaspoon salt
½ teaspoon instant beef bouillon granules
¼ teaspoon ground ginger
1 cup quick-cooking rice
2 smoked pork chops, cut ½ inch thick
2 tablespoons apricot preserves

Drain pineapple, reserving syrup. Set aside 1 pineapple slice; chop the remaining pineapple. Add enough water to reserved syrup to make ¾ cup liquid.

In an 8-inch skillet combine the pineapple syrup, green pepper, 2 tablespoons apricot preserves, salt, bouillon granules, and ginger. Stir in rice and chopped pineapple. Bring to boiling. Place chops atop rice.

Quarter the reserved pineapple slice; arrange atop pork chops. Reduce heat and simmer, covered, for 15 to 18 minutes or till rice is tender. Spoon the remaining 2 tablespoons apricot preserves atop pork chops and pineapple. Makes 2 servings. (Adaptable for one.)†

Mexicali Pork Chops

2 pork loin chops, cut ¾ inch thick
1 tablespoon shortening
¼ cup chopped green pepper
2 tablespoons chopped onion
1 8-ounce can tomatoes, cut up
1 8-ounce can red kidney beans
¼ cup long grain rice
¼ cup water
½ of a 4-ounce can green chili peppers, rinsed, seeded, and chopped
½ teaspoon salt
Paprika
Sliced pitted ripe olives (optional)
Parsley sprigs (optional)

In skillet brown chops on both sides in hot shortening. Sprinkle with a little salt and pepper. Remove chops from skillet. Reserve drippings in skillet.

Cook green pepper and onion in reserved drippings till tender. Stir in tomatoes, kidney beans, rice, water, chilies, and salt. Bring to boiling. Turn mixture into a 10×6×2-inch baking dish.

Arrange the pork chops atop tomato-rice mixture. Bake, covered, in 350° oven about 50 minutes or till meat is tender. Sprinkle chops with paprika. If desired, garnish with olives and parsley before serving. Makes 2 servings. (Adaptable for one.)†

When browning pork chops, you may use the trimmings from the chops instead of 1 tablespoon shortening.

Trim the excess fat from chops and heat in skillet till 1 tablespoon accumulates. Discard trimmings.

†See page 3 for directions.

Pork four-way dinners

For **Basic Pork Mixture** cut 2½ pounds boneless pork into ¾-inch cubes. In large skillet brown meat, half at a time, in 2 tablespoons cooking oil. Return all meat to skillet. Stir in 1 cup chopped onion; 1 cup water; 1 clove garlic, minced; and ¾ teaspoon salt. Bring to boiling., Reduce heat; simmer, covered, 50 to 60 minutes or till tender. Chill. When cold, skim fat from surface; discard fat. Spoon mixture into four 1-cup freezer containers. Seal, label, and freeze. Use in pork recipes on the next page. Makes about 4 cups.

Barbecued Pork

Pork Stroganoff

Herbed Pork Stew

Pork Oriental Toss

Pork Oriental Toss

1 container (1 cup) frozen *Basic Pork Mixture*
½ cup water
3 tablespoons soy sauce
1 teaspoon instant beef bouillon granules
1 cup bias-sliced celery
½ of a 6-ounce package (1 cup) frozen pea pods, partially thawed
⅓ cup water chestnuts, drained and sliced
1 2½-ounce jar sliced mushrooms, drained
4 teaspoons cornstarch
4 teaspoons cold water
  Hot cooked rice
1 tablespoon sliced almonds, toasted

In saucepan combine frozen pork mixture, the ½ cup water, soy sauce, and beef bouillon granules. Cover and cook over low heat about 15 minutes or till thawed, stirring occasionally to break up pork mixture.

Add celery, pea pods, water chestnuts, and mushrooms. Cover and simmer for 2 minutes.

Blend cornstarch and the 4 teaspoons cold water; stir into pork mixture. Cook and stir till thickened and bubbly. Serve with rice. Sprinkle with toasted almonds. Makes 2 servings.

Herbed Pork Stew

1 container (1 cup) frozen *Basic Pork Mixture*
1 small bay leaf
¼ teaspoon dried rosemary, crushed
¼ teaspoon dried thyme, crushed
2 medium carrots, sliced
2 small potatoes, peeled and cut up
2 tablespoons all-purpose flour

Combine pork mixture, bay leaf, herbs, ¾ cup *water*, ¾ teaspoon *salt*, and ⅛ teaspoon *pepper*. Cover and cook over low heat about 15 minutes or till thawed; stir occasionally. Add vegetables; cover and simmer 15 to 20 minutes or till tender. Blend ¼ cup cold *water* and flour; stir into pork mixture. Cook and stir till thick and bubbly. Serves 2.

Barbecued Pork

1 container (1 cup) frozen *Basic Pork Mixture*
½ cup tomato sauce
2 tablespoons sliced green onion
1 tablespoon brown sugar
2 teaspoons prepared mustard
1½ teaspoons worcestershire sauce
¼ teaspoon chili powder
1 teaspoon cornstarch
2 kaiser rolls *or* hamburger buns, split and toasted

Combine pork and next 6 ingredients. Cover and cook over low heat about 15 minutes or till thawed; stir occasionally. Uncover; cook and stir 5 to 10 minutes. Blend cornstarch and 1 teaspoon cold *water;* stir into pork mixture. Cook and stir till bubbly. Serve in rolls or buns. Serves 2.

Pork Stroganoff

1 container (1 cup) frozen *Basic Pork Mixture*
⅓ cup water
3 tablespoons dry white wine
1 tablespoon catsup
½ teaspoon instant beef bouillon granules
4 teaspoons all-purpose flour
⅓ cup dairy sour cream
1½ cups hot cooked noodles
½ teaspoon poppy seed
  Lemon slices (optional)

In saucepan combine frozen pork mixture, water, white wine, catsup, and beef bouillon granules. Cover and cook over low heat about 15 minutes or till thawed, stirring occasionally to break up pork mixture.

Blend flour into sour cream. Stir about 1 cup of the hot pork mixture into sour cream mixture; return to remaining hot pork mixture in saucepan. Cook over low heat, stirring constantly, till mixture is slightly thickened; *do not boil.*

Stir together cooked noodles and poppy seed; spoon onto serving platter. Top with pork mixture. Arrange lemon slices atop, if desired. Makes 2 servings.

Coconut Pork Kabob

2 tablespoons grated coconut
1 tablespoon peanut butter
1 tablespoon soy sauce
2 teaspoons honey
¼ teaspoon lemon juice *or* lime juice
⅛ teaspoon ground ginger
  Dash bottled hot pepper sauce
¼ pound lean boneless pork, cut into 1-inch pieces

In small bowl combine coconut, peanut butter, soy sauce, honey, lemon or lime juice, ginger, and pepper sauce. Set aside.

Thread pork on a 10-inch skewer. Place on unheated rack in broiler pan. Broil 3 to 4 inches from heat about 12 minutes or till pork is nearly done, turning skewer occasionally.

Brush coconut mixture over meat. Broil about 3 minutes more or till golden brown, turning skewer often. Makes 1 serving.

Prepare a small roast when you want to enjoy roast pork without having more leftovers than you can readily use.

To roast a 3-pound pork center loin roast, sprinkle with salt and pepper. Place meat, fat side up, on rack in shallow roasting pan. Insert a meat thermometer into center of meat. Roast in 325° oven for 1½ to 1¾ hours or till thermometer registers 170°. Let roast stand about 15 minutes for easier carving.

Grilled Chinese Pork Tenderloin

1 ¾-pound pork tenderloin
¼ cup catsup
2 tablespoons dry sherry
2 tablespoons soy sauce
1 tablespoon honey
1 tablespoon vinegar
¼ teaspoon garlic powder

Place meat in a plastic bag; set in shallow pan. For marinade combine catsup, sherry, soy sauce, honey, vinegar, and garlic powder; pour over meat. Close bag; marinate 2 to 4 hours in the refrigerator, turning meat occasionally. Drain meat, reserving the marinade.

Place meat on grill over *slow* coals. Grill meat for ¾ to 1 hour or till nearly done, turning occasionally. Brush with reserved marinade and continue grilling about 15 minutes or till glazed, turning and brushing with marinade every 5 minutes.

Before serving, check for doneness by making a small slit in the thickest part of the meat. It should not be pink.

(*Or,* to roast meat instead of grilling it, place meat on a rack in shallow roasting pan. Insert meat thermometer into center of meat. Roast in 325° oven for ¾ to 1 hour or till thermometer registers 170°, brushing occasionally with reserved marinade the last 15 minutes.) Makes 2 large servings.

Deviled Barbecued Ribs

2 pounds pork spareribs
1 tablespoon butter
1 tablespoon chopped onion
1 tablespoon chopped green pepper
1 clove garlic, minced
⅓ cup chili sauce
1 tablespoon brown sugar
2 teaspoons worcestershire sauce
1 teaspoon dry mustard
½ teaspoon celery seed
  Few drops bottled hot pepper sauce
2 thin lemon slices

Cut ribs into serving-size pieces. In saucepan pour enough water over ribs to cover. Bring to boiling; reduce heat. Cover and simmer about 45 minutes or till nearly tender. Drain well.

For sauce melt butter. Add onion, green pepper, and garlic. Stir in chili sauce, brown sugar, worcestershire, mustard, celery seed, pepper sauce, ¼ teaspoon *salt,* and dash *pepper.* Add lemon slices; bring to boiling.

Place ribs in a shallow baking pan. Spoon some sauce over ribs. Bake in 350° oven about 20 minutes, basting occasionally with remaining sauce. Serves 2.

Microwave cooking directions: Cut ribs into serving-size pieces; set aside. For sauce, in small nonmetal bowl combine butter, onion, green pepper, and garlic. Cook, uncovered, in countertop microwave oven on high power about 1½ minutes or till tender. Stir in remaining ingredients, ¼ teaspoon *salt,* and dash *pepper.*

Arrange ribs in 12×7½×2-inch nonmetal baking dish. Micro-cook, covered with waxed paper, 20 minutes; give dish a half turn after 10 minutes. Pour off fat. Pour sauce atop. Micro-cook, covered, about 10 minutes; give dish a half turn after 5 minutes.

Tangy Pork Cabbage Rolls

1 head cabbage
1 beaten egg
3 tablespoons finely chopped onion
1 tablespoon snipped parsley
½ teaspoon salt
½ teaspoon worcestershire sauce
 Dash pepper
½ pound ground pork
½ cup cooked rice
1 8-ounce can tomato sauce
2 tablespoons raisins (optional)
2 tablespoons brown sugar
2 tablespoons vinegar

Remove 4 large outer leaves from cabbage; set aside. Shred enough of the remaining cabbage to make 2 cups. Place the 2 cups shredded cabbage in bottom of a 10×6×2-inch baking dish. Immerse the reserved cabbage leaves in boiling water about 3 minutes or just till limp; drain. Cut about 2 inches of heavy center vein out of cabbage leaves. Sprinkle generously with salt.

In mixing bowl combine beaten egg, onion, parsley, salt, worcestershire sauce, and pepper. Add ground pork and cooked rice; mix well.

Place ¼ of the meat mixture in center of each leaf; fold in sides. Fold ends so they overlap atop meat mixture. Place rolls, seam side down, atop cabbage in baking dish. Combine tomato sauce, raisins, brown sugar, and vinegar. Pour over cabbage. Bake, covered, in 350° oven for 1 to 1¼ hours. Makes 2 servings.

Cherry Glaze for Ham

¼ cup cherry preserves
2 teaspoons prepared mustard
 Dash ground cloves

For glaze combine cherry preserves, mustard, and cloves.

To glaze a small fully cooked ham, refer to tip at right. At the last 15 minutes of baking time for ham, spoon fat from pan. Spoon about half the glaze over ham. Continue baking about 15 minutes or till meat thermometer registers 140°, spooning remaining glaze over after 10 minutes. Makes ¼ cup glaze.

Ham with Rye Stuffing

2 tablespoons finely chopped onion
2 tablespoons butter or margarine
2 to 3 tablespoons orange juice*
½ teaspoon prepared mustard
⅛ teaspoon caraway seed
 Dash pepper
3 slices rye bread, cubed
1 ¾-pound fully cooked ham slice, cut ½ inch thick

In saucepan cook onion in butter or margarine till tender but not brown. Blend in orange juice, mustard, caraway seed, and pepper. Add bread; toss lightly.

Cut ham slice into quarters. Spread bread mixture over 2 of the ham quarters. Top with remaining 2 ham quarters; secure with wooden picks. Place in an 8×8×2-inch baking dish. Bake, covered, in 375° oven for 20 to 25 minutes or till heated through. Makes 2 servings. (Adaptable for one.)†

*Use the larger amount of orange juice for a moist stuffing.

†See page 3 for directions.

Bake a small ham portion or canned ham when you want to enjoy ham without having a lot of leftovers.

Fully cooked hams are completely cooked and ready-to-eat, but may be heated before serving, if desired. To bake a 1- to 1½-pound fully cooked boneless smoked ham portion, place ham, fat side up, on a rack in small shallow baking pan. Score ham fat in diamonds, cutting only ¼ inch deep. Insert a meat thermometer into center of meat, making sure bulb does not rest in fat. Bake, uncovered, in 325° oven about 45 minutes or till meat thermometer registers 140°.

Hams that are not labeled "fully cooked" need additional baking to finish cooking and develop flavors. They must be cooked to an internal temperature of 160° before eating.

Ham Hawaiian

1 medium sweet potato *or* yam
½ of a medium pineapple *or* 1
  8¼-ounce can pineapple
  chunks, drained
¼ teaspoon instant chicken
  bouillon granules
¼ cup water
2 slices fully cooked ham
  (about ½ pound)
1 small orange, halved and
  thinly sliced
½ of a 6-ounce package (1 cup)
  frozen pea pods, thawed
¼ cup orange marmalade
1 tablespoon butter *or*
  margarine

In covered pan cook sweet potato in enough boiling salted water to cover about 30 minutes or just till tender. Peel; halve lengthwise and crosswise. Cut fresh pineapple into chunks, removing core. In small wok or 10-inch skillet dissolve chicken bouillon granules in water. Place a small heat-proof trivet or rack over liquid in pan.

Arrange sweet potato, fresh or canned pineapple, ham slices, and orange slices on rack. Cover tightly with lid or foil. Set wok on wok holder directly in *medium-slow* coals *or* on range over medium-high heat. (Set skillet on grill over *medium-slow* coals *or* on range over medium heat.) Steam for 15 minutes. Remove cover. Add thawed pea pods. Replace cover and steam 15 to 20 minutes more.

In saucepan combine orange marmalade and butter or margarine. Cook and stir till heated through. Drizzle over ham mixture. Makes 2 servings.

Ham Patties with Sour Cream-Onion Sauce

1 beaten egg
¼ cup fine dry bread crumbs
1 tablespoon catsup
¼ teaspoon dried oregano,
  crushed
¼ teaspoon dried basil,
  crushed
⅛ teaspoon pepper
½ pound ground fully cooked
  ham
1 slice mozzarella *or* Swiss
  cheese, torn up (1½
  ounces)
¼ cup sliced fresh mushrooms
½ small onion, sliced
1 tablespoon butter *or*
  margarine
1½ teaspoons all-purpose flour
¼ cup water
1 tablespoоon snipped
  parsley
1 tablespoon dry sherry
¼ cup dairy sour cream

In mixing bowl combine egg, bread crumbs, catsup, oregano, basil, and pepper. Add ground ham; mix well. Shape into four 3½-inch-diameter patties. Place cheese atop 2 patties; cover with remaining 2 patties. Seal edges. Place in a 10×6×2-inch baking dish. Bake in 350° oven about 40 minutes or till done.

In small saucepan cook mushrooms and onion in butter or margarine till tender. Blend in flour; stir in water, parsley, and sherry. Cook and stir till thickened and bubbly. Blend in sour cream and heat through; *do not boil.* Season to taste with salt. Serve over ham patties. Makes 2 servings.

Ham Fried Rice

2 beaten eggs
2 tablespoons cooking oil
1 cup finely chopped fully
  cooked ham
1 2-ounce can chopped
  mushrooms, drained
3 tablespoons sliced green
  onion
1 tablespoon soy sauce
1 clove garlic, minced
⅛ teaspoon ground ginger
1½ cups cold cooked rice*

In 10-inch skillet cook eggs in *1 tablespoon* of the oil, without stirring, till set. Invert skillet over a baking sheet to remove cooked eggs; cut eggs into short narrow strips.

In same skillet cook chopped ham, mushrooms, green onion, soy sauce, garlic, and ginger in the remaining oil over high heat for 3 to 4 minutes. Stir in *cold* cooked rice and egg strips; heat through. Pass additional soy sauce, if desired. Makes 2 servings. (Adaptable for one.)†

Chill rice before preparing this dish. Using hot cooked rice causes the mixture to stick.

Mustard-Glazed Canadian Bacon

2 ¼-inch-thick slices
  Canadian-style bacon
1 tablespoon brown sugar
1 tablespoon orange juice
½ teaspoon prepared mustard
  Dash ground cloves

In small skillet lightly brown bacon on both sides.

For glaze stir together brown sugar, orange juice, mustard, and cloves. Spoon over bacon. Cover and cook about 5 minutes, basting once. Transfer bacon to plate and spoon the glaze over meat. Makes 1 serving.

†See page 3 for directions.

Festive Ham Hawaiian *features ham slices, sweet potato, pineapple, orange slices, and pea pods accented with tangy orange marmalade.*

Lamb

Lamb with Peaches

½ pound boneless lamb, cut into ¾-inch cubes
1 tablespoon butter *or* margarine
½ teaspoon salt
¼ teaspoon ground cinnamon
⅛ teaspoon ground nutmeg
    Dash pepper
1 8¾-ounce can peach slices
½ cup water
2 tablespoons raisins
2 tablespoons chopped walnuts
1 tablespoon snipped parsley
2 tablespoons cold water
1½ teaspoons cornstarch
    Hot cooked rice

In 8-inch skillet brown lamb in butter or margarine. Add salt, cinnamon, nutmeg, and pepper. Drain peach slices, reserving syrup. Stir the reserved peach syrup, ½ cup water, raisins, walnuts, and parsley into lamb. Cover and simmer for 1 to 1¼ hours or till lamb is tender.

Blend 2 tablespoons cold water and cornstarch; stir into lamb mixture. Cook and stir till mixture is thickened and bubbly. Add sliced peaches and heat through. Serve over hot cooked rice. Makes 2 servings.

Herbed Lamb Stew

½ pound boneless lamb*, cut into ¾-inch cubes
1 tablespoon cooking oil
1 cup water
1 clove garlic, minced
1 small bay leaf
1 teaspoon instant beef bouillon granules
¼ teaspoon salt
¼ teaspoon dried oregano, crushed
¼ teaspoon dried thyme, crushed
¼ teaspoon dried marjoram, crushed
⅛ teaspoon pepper
2 medium carrots, cut into ½-inch pieces (1 cup)
2 stalks celery, cut into 1-inch pieces (1 cup)
1 small onion, cut into thin wedges
¼ cup dairy sour cream
2 tablespoons all-purpose flour
1 tablespoon water

In 2-quart saucepan brown meat in hot oil; remove from heat. Add the 1 cup water, garlic, bay leaf, bouillon granules, salt, oregano, thyme, marjoram, and pepper. Bring mixture to boiling; reduce heat and simmer, covered, for 25 minutes. Add carrots, celery, and onion. Cover and simmer about 25 minutes more or till meat and vegetables are tender. Remove bay leaf.

Combine sour cream, flour, and the 1 tablespoon water. Blend about ½ cup of the hot mixture into sour cream mixture; return to remaining hot mixture. Cook and stir till thickened and bubbly. Makes 2 servings.

Stew is equally tasty made with boneless beef.

Tender cubes of lamb cooked with vegetables in a rich and creamy sauce make Herbed Lamb Stew a hearty favorite of lamb lovers!

Stir-Fried Lamb and Asparagus

½ pound boneless lamb
2 tablespoons soy sauce
1 teaspoon cornstarch
1 tablespoon lemon juice
1 tablespoon dry sherry
1 tablespoon water
¼ teaspoon instant beef bouillon granules
⅛ teaspoon crushed aniseed
2 tablespoons cooking oil
1 cup fresh asparagus bias-sliced into 1-inch lengths*
4 green onions, bias-sliced into 1-inch lengths
1 cup fresh *or* canned bean sprouts

Partially freeze lamb. Slice thinly into bite-size strips. In small mixing bowl blend soy sauce and cornstarch; stir in lemon juice, sherry, water, beef bouillon granules, and aniseed. Set aside.

Preheat a wok or skillet over high heat; add cooking oil. Add sliced asparagus; cook and stir for 1 minute. Add green onions; cook and stir about 2 minutes or till crisp-tender. Remove vegetables. (Add more cooking oil, if necessary.)

Add lamb to *hot* wok or skillet; cook and stir about 3 minutes or till just browned. Stir soy mixture, then stir into lamb. Cook and stir till thickened and bubbly. Stir in asparagus, green onions, and bean sprouts. Cover and cook for 1 minute. Serve at once. Makes 2 servings. (Adaptable for one.)†

If fresh asparagus isn't available, substitute 1 cup frozen cut asparagus.

Spiced Lamb Kabobs

2 small carrots, cut into 1-inch pieces
1 medium onion, cut into wedges
2 tablespoons chopped onion
2 tablespoons water
¼ cup chili sauce
1 tablespoon brown sugar
1 tablespoon vinegar
¼ teaspoon salt
¼ teaspoon ground cinnamon
⅛ teaspoon ground coriander
Dash bottled hot pepper sauce
½ pound boneless lamb, cut into 1-inch pieces

In covered saucepan cook carrot pieces in boiling salted water for 8 minutes. Add onion wedges; cook about 3 minutes longer or till vegetables are nearly tender. Drain.

For basting sauce, in small covered saucepan cook the chopped onion in 2 tablespoons water about 5 minutes or till tender. Stir in chili sauce, brown sugar, vinegar, salt, cinnamon, coriander, and pepper sauce.

Alternately thread lamb, carrots, and onion wedges on 2 long skewers. Place on unheated rack in broiler pan. Broil about 4 inches from heat for 10 to 12 minutes, turning and brushing occasionally with basting sauce. Makes 2 servings. (Adaptable for one.)†

Deviled Lamb Chop

1 lamb shoulder chop
1 tablespoon cooking oil
2 tablespoons water
2 teaspoons prepared mustard
½ teaspoon lemon juice
⅛ teaspoon dried thyme, crushed
Dash garlic salt
1 onion slice
2 ½-inch-thick green pepper rings

Sprinkle meat lightly with salt and pepper. Brown chop in hot oil. Combine water, mustard, lemon juice, thyme, and garlic salt. Spread mustard mixture over chop; top with onion slice.

Cover and simmer for 15 minutes. Spoon pan juices over lamb chop; top with green pepper rings. Cover and simmer about 15 minutes more or till meat is tender. Makes 1 serving.

Mixed Grill

2 lamb loin chops, cut ¾ inch thick
⅛ teaspoon dried basil, crushed
⅛ teaspoon dried oregano, crushed
4 brown-and-serve sausage links
1 small tomato, quartered
1 small green pepper, cut into rings

Preheat griddle or electric skillet to 375°; grease lightly. Cook chops on griddle or in skillet 6 to 7 minutes. Turn; sprinkle with basil and oregano. Season with a little salt and pepper. Add sausages, tomato, and green pepper. Cook about 7 minutes or till lamb is done, turning sausages and vegetables occasionally. Makes 2 servings. (Adaptable for one.)†

Lamb Shanks in Spicy Tomato Sauce

2 lamb shanks (1¾ to 2 pounds total)
1 tablespoon cooking oil
½ medium onion, sliced (¼ cup)
¼ cup sliced celery
1 8-ounce can tomato sauce
1 small clove garlic, minced
½ teaspoon chili powder
¼ teaspoon salt
   Dash bottled hot pepper sauce
   Hot cooked noodles

Sprinkle the lamb shanks with a little salt and pepper. In a 10-inch skillet brown the lamb shanks on all sides in hot cooking oil. Add sliced onion and sliced celery.

Stir together tomato sauce, garlic, chili powder, salt, and bottled hot pepper sauce. Pour the tomato sauce mixture over lamb shanks in skillet. Cover and simmer about 1½ hours or till meat is tender.

Place lamb shanks atop hot cooked noodles. Skim excess fat from tomato sauce mixture; spoon the mixture over lamb shanks and noodles. Makes 2 servings.

Individual Glazed Lamb Loaves

1 beaten egg
½ cup soft bread crumbs
2 tablespoons finely chopped onion
½ teaspoon salt
½ teaspoon finely shredded orange peel
¼ teaspoon dried mint flakes
⅛ teaspoon dried rosemary, crushed
   Dash pepper
¾ pound ground lamb
2 tablespoons honey
1 tablespoon orange juice

In mixing bowl combine egg, bread crumbs, onion, salt, ¼ teaspoon of the orange peel, mint flakes, rosemary, and pepper. Add ground lamb; mix well. Shape into two 4½×2½-inch loaves. Place in small shallow baking pan. Bake in 350° oven for 30 minutes.

Meanwhile, for glaze combine honey, orange juice, and the remaining ¼ teaspoon orange peel. Brush half the glaze over meat loaves. Bake about 10 minutes longer. Brush with remaining glaze. Makes 2 servings.

Microwave cooking directions: Prepare meat mixture as above. In 9-inch nonmetal pie plate shape mixture into two 4½×2½-inch loaves. Cook, covered with waxed paper, in countertop microwave oven on high power for 7 to 8 minutes, giving dish a quarter turn 3 times.

For glaze combine honey, orange juice, and the remaining ¼ teaspoon orange peel. Brush half the glaze over loaves. Micro-cook, uncovered, about 1 minute longer or till meat is done. Brush with remaining glaze.

Lamb Patties with Creamed Peas and Onion

2 tablespoons milk
2 tablespoons catsup
⅓ cup soft bread crumbs (½ slice)
¼ teaspoon salt
¼ teaspoon dried marjoram, crushed
   Dash pepper
½ pound ground lamb
1 tablespoon cooking oil
½ medium onion, thinly sliced and separated into rings
1 tablespoon butter *or* margarine
1 teaspoon all-purpose flour
¼ cup milk
1 8½-ounce can peas, drained
⅛ teaspoon salt
   Dash pepper

In mixing bowl combine the 2 tablespoons milk, catsup, bread crumbs, ¼ teaspoon salt, marjoram, and dash pepper. Add ground lamb; mix well. Shape into two ¾-inch-thick patties.

In an 8-inch skillet cook patties in hot oil over medium heat for 5 to 6 minutes on each side or till done. Remove patties; drain fat.

In same skillet cook onion in butter or margarine till tender but not brown. Blend in flour; add ¼ cup milk all at once. Stir in peas, ⅛ teaspoon salt, and dash pepper. Cook and stir till thickened and bubbly. Return patties to skillet. Cover; heat through. Makes 2 servings. (Adaptable for one.)†

†See page 3 for directions.

Sausages & Franks

Apple-Sausage Curry

1 medium apple, peeled, cored, and chopped (¾ cup)
½ medium onion, chopped (¼ cup)
1 to 1½ teaspoons curry powder*
1 tablespoon butter *or* margarine
¾ cup cold water
2 teaspoons cornstarch
1 teaspoon instant chicken bouillon granules
1 6-ounce piece ring bologna, sliced (1 cup)
2 tablespoons raisins
Hot cooked rice
Shredded coconut (optional)
Chopped peanuts (optional)

In small covered skillet cook apple, onion, and curry powder in butter or margarine till apple and onion are tender. Blend water and cornstarch. Stir cornstarch mixture and chicken bouillon granules into curry mixture in skillet. Cook, stirring constantly, till thickened and bubbly.

Add sliced bologna and raisins. Cook, uncovered, over low heat about 5 minutes or till sausage is heated through. Serve curry mixture over hot cooked rice. Sprinkle with shredded coconut and/or chopped peanuts, if desired. Makes 2 servings. (Adaptable for one.)†

Use the smaller amount of curry powder if you prefer mildly seasoned food.

Sweet-Sour Bratwurst Skillet

2 tablespoons brown sugar
2 tablespoons vinegar
2 tablespoons water
½ teaspoon prepared mustard
¼ teaspoon salt
⅛ teaspoon garlic powder
Dash pepper
1 8-ounce can sauerkraut, drained
1 medium apple, cored and cut into wedges
¼ cup chopped sweet red *or* green pepper
2 tablespoons sliced green onion
4 fully cooked smoked bratwurst *or* Polish sausage links
Snipped parsley (optional)

In skillet combine brown sugar, vinegar, water, mustard, salt, garlic powder, and pepper. Stir in sauerkraut, apple wedges, red or green pepper, and onion.

Score sausage links by making crosswise slits at 1-inch intervals, almost to the opposite side. Place sausages atop sauerkraut mixture. Cover and simmer for 10 to 15 minutes or till apple is tender and sausages are heated through. Sprinkle with parsley, if desired. Makes 2 servings. (Adaptable for one.)†

†See page 3 for directions.

The sweet and tangy flavors of apple and sauerkraut team up with smoky bratwurst to make quick fixin' Sweet-Sour Bratwurst Skillet.

Hearty Italian Sausage Lasagna

3 ounces lasagna noodles (4 or 5 noodles)
½ pound bulk Italian sausage
2 tablespoons chopped onion
1 8-ounce can tomato sauce
1 large tomato, peeled and coarsely chopped
1 clove garlic, minced
¼ teaspoon dried basil, crushed
¼ teaspoon dried oregano, crushed
⅛ teaspoon pepper
   Dash salt
1 beaten egg
½ cup ricotta *or* cream-style cottage cheese
2 tablespoons grated parmesan cheese
2 tablespoons snipped parsley
¼ cup shredded mozzarella cheese (1 ounce)

Cook lasagna noodles according to package directions; drain. Halve noodles crosswise. In skillet cook sausage and onion till meat is browned and onion is tender; drain off fat.

Combine tomato sauce, chopped tomato, garlic, basil, oregano, pepper, and salt; add to meat and mix well. In small mixing bowl combine egg, ricotta or cottage cheese, grated parmesan cheese, and parsley.

Place *half* the noodles in a greased 6½×6½×2-inch baking dish (*or* place ¼ of the noodles in each of 2 greased 5×5×2-inch baking dishes). Spread *half* the sausage mixture atop noodles. Spoon the egg-cheese mixture over sausage layer. Top with remaining noodles. Spread remaining sausage mixture over noodles; sprinkle with mozzarella cheese. Bake, covered, in 375° oven for 30 to 35 minutes. Let stand 10 minutes before serving. Makes 2 servings.

Sausage-Lima Skillet

1 beaten egg
2 tablespoons fine dry bread crumbs
2 tablespoons chopped onion
2 tablespoons chopped green pepper
¼ teaspoon dried marjoram, crushed
½ pound bulk pork sausage
1 tablespoon all-purpose flour
¼ cup dry white wine
½ teaspoon liquid beef-flavored gravy base
1 8½-ounce can lima beans, drained

Combine first 5 ingredients and ¼ teaspoon *salt*. Add meat; mix well. Shape into 12 to 14 meatballs. Brown on all sides; set aside. Drain off fat, reserving 1 tablespoon drippings. Stir flour into reserved drippings. Add wine, gravy base, ¾ cup *water*, and dash *pepper*. Cook and stir till bubbly. Add meatballs and limas. Simmer, covered, 10 to 15 minutes. Makes 2 servings.

Sausage Mac

¾ cup elbow macaroni
½ pound bulk pork sausage
¼ cup chopped onion
½ cup canned whole kernel corn
1 tablespoon snipped parsley
1 3-ounce package cream cheese, softened
⅔ cup milk

Cook macaroni in boiling salted water about 8 minutes or till just tender; drain. Cook meat and onion till meat is browned; drain fat. Add corn, parsley, ¼ teaspoon *salt*, and ⅛ teaspoon *pepper*; stir in cream cheese and milk. Stir in macaroni and heat through. Makes 2 servings. (Adaptable for one.)†

Sausage Cornbread Casserole

¼ cup all-purpose flour
¼ cup yellow cornmeal
1 teaspoon sugar
½ teaspoon baking powder
¼ teaspoon salt
1 8¾-ounce can cream-style corn
1 slightly beaten egg
1 tablespoon milk
4 brown-and-serve sausage links
¼ cup shredded Swiss cheese (1 ounce)
   Parsley sprigs (optional)

In mixing bowl combine flour, yellow cornmeal, sugar, baking powder, and salt. Stir in cream-style corn, egg, and milk. Turn cornmeal mixture into two 10-ounce casseroles.

Halve sausage links crosswise. Arrange 4 of the unbrowned sausage halves atop each casserole. Bake in 350° oven for 25 to 30 minutes.

Sprinkle each casserole with half the Swiss cheese. Return to oven and bake about 5 minutes longer or till knife inserted in center comes out clean. Garnish with parsley sprigs, if desired. Makes 2 servings.

Pepperoni-Green Pepper Pan Pizza

1 package active dry yeast
⅓ cup warm water (110°)
1½ cups packaged biscuit mix
    Yellow cornmeal
¾ cup shredded mozzarella
    cheese (3 ounces)
1 small green pepper,
    chopped (½ cup)
½ cup tomato sauce
¼ teaspoon dried basil,
    crushed
2 ounces sliced pepperoni

In mixing bowl soften yeast in warm water. Stir in biscuit mix. Cover and let rest 10 minutes.

Grease a heavy 8-inch skillet with oven-proof handle; sprinkle bottom with a little yellow cornmeal. With greased fingers, pat dough out onto bottom and halfway up sides of skillet. Bake in 400° oven for 10 to 15 minutes or till lightly browned.

Sprinkle baked crust with *half* the mozzarella cheese. In small mixing bowl combine green pepper, tomato sauce, and basil; spoon over cheese-topped crust in skillet. Top with pepperoni slices and remaining cheese. Bake in 400° oven about 15 minutes longer. To serve, cut into wedges. Makes 2 servings.

Bacon-Wrapped Stuffed Frank

1 large frankfurter
1 tablespoon finely chopped
    onion
2 tablespoons water
2 tablespoons seasoned
    croutons
2 tablespoons shredded
    sharp American cheese
1½ teaspoons sweet pickle
    relish
1 slice bacon

Cut frank lengthwise almost to opposite side; set aside. In small covered saucepan cook onion in water about 5 minutes or till tender. Add croutons, tossing lightly to mix. Stir in *half* of the American cheese and the pickle relish. Mound crouton mixture inside frank.

Place bacon on unheated rack in broiler pan. Broil about 4 inches from heat about 1½ minutes or till partially cooked. Drain on paper toweling. Wrap stuffed frank with the strip of partially cooked bacon; secure with wooden picks.

Place frank, cut side up, on unheated rack in broiler pan. Broil about 4 inches from heat for 2 minutes. Turn, cut side down, and broil about 2 minutes or just till bacon is crisp. Turn, cut side up; sprinkle with the remaining cheese. Broil about 30 seconds more or till cheese melts. Makes 1 serving.

Hungarian Frankfurters

1 cup medium noodles
2 cups chopped cabbage
2 tablespoons chopped onion
1 tablespoon snipped parsley
¼ teaspoon salt
¼ teaspoon dry mustard
⅛ teaspoon pepper
1 tablespoon cooking oil
½ cup milk
3 or 4 frankfurters, cut
    crosswise into fourths
1 tablespoon all-purpose flour
½ cup dairy sour cream
2 tablespoons grated
    parmesan cheese
    Paprika

In saucepan cook noodles in boiling salted water about 8 minutes or till just tender; drain. In covered skillet cook chopped cabbage, onion, parsley, salt, mustard, and pepper in hot cooking oil about 10 minutes or till vegetables are tender. Stir in milk; add cut-up frankfurters. Cover and simmer about 5 minutes or till franks are heated through.

Blend flour into sour cream; stir sour cream mixture and cooked noodles into cabbage mixture. Cook and stir till thickened and bubbly. Sprinkle with parmesan cheese and a little paprika. Makes 2 servings. (Adaptable for one.)†

†See page 3 for directions.

Fish & Seafood

Sole Provençal

2 fresh *or* frozen sole fillets *or* other fish fillets (½ to ¾ pound total)
1 tablespoon butter *or* margarine
Salt
Paprika
1 medium tomato, peeled, cored, and cut up
¼ cup sliced fresh mushrooms *or* 1 2-ounce can chopped mushrooms, drained
2 tablespoons sliced green onion
2 tablespoons snipped parsley
2 tablespoons dry white wine
1 clove garlic, minced
⅛ teaspoon salt
Lemon wedges (optional)
Parsley sprigs (optional)

Thaw fish, if frozen. Dot fillets with butter or margarine. Sprinkle with a little salt and paprika. Roll up fish fillets and fasten with wooden picks.

Place fillet rolls in 8-inch skillet. Add tomato, mushrooms, green onion, snipped parsley, white wine, garlic, and the ⅛ teaspoon salt. Cover tightly and simmer for 7 to 8 minutes or till fish flakes easily when tested with a fork. Remove fish to warm platter; keep warm.

Uncover skillet and boil tomato mixture for 2 to 3 minutes or till slightly thickened. Spoon tomato mixture over fish rolls. Garnish with lemon wedges and parsley sprigs, if desired. Makes 2 servings. (Adaptable for one.)†

Wild Rice-Stuffed Red Snapper

1 1½-pound fresh *or* frozen dressed red snapper *or* other fish (with head and tail)
½ of a 4-ounce package (⅓ cup) wild rice
½ cup sliced fresh mushrooms
2 tablespoons butter
½ cup frozen peas, thawed
½ teaspoon finely shredded lemon peel
2 tablespoons lemon juice
1 tablespoon sliced green onion
1 tablespoon chopped pimiento
2 tablespoons butter, melted
2 tablespoons lemon juice

Thaw fish, if frozen. Cook rice according to package directions. Cook mushrooms in 2 tablespoons butter till tender. For stuffing combine cooked rice, cooked mushrooms, peas, lemon peel, 2 tablespoons lemon juice, green onion, pimiento, ½ teaspoon *salt*, and ⅛ teaspoon *pepper*. Toss lightly.

Sprinkle fish inside and out with salt. Fill fish cavity with stuffing, patting stuffing to flatten evenly. Tie or skewer fish closed; place in a greased shallow baking dish.

For basting sauce combine 2 tablespoons melted butter and 2 tablespoons lemon juice. Brush some over fish. Bake in 350° oven for 30 to 35 minutes or till fish flakes easily when tested with a fork, brushing occasionally with remaining basting sauce. Carefully lift fish to warm platter. Remove strings or skewers; remove stuffing from cavity. Garnish with lemon slices and bias-sliced green onions, if desired. Makes 2 servings.

†See page 3 for directions.

Savor fresh-from-the-sea Wild Rice-Stuffed Red Snapper *that combines the delicate tang of lemon with wild rice, mushrooms, peas, onion, and pimiento.*

Barbecued Bass Steaks

2 fresh *or* frozen bass steaks
   or other fish steaks (about
   12 ounces)
3 tablespoons catsup
1 tablespoon lemon juice
1 tablespoon soy sauce
2 teaspoons cooking oil
½ teaspoon sugar
¼ teaspoon salt
⅛ teaspoon garlic powder
   Dash cayenne

Thaw fish, if frozen. Place fish in a plastic bag; set in shallow pan. For marinade combine catsup, lemon juice, soy sauce, cooking oil, sugar, salt, garlic powder, and cayenne. Pour marinade over fish; close bag. Marinate about 30 minutes at room temperature, turning fish once or twice. Remove fish, reserving marinade.

Place fish steaks in a well-greased wire grill basket. Grill over *medium-hot* coals for 8 minutes. Turn fish and baste with some of the reserved marinade. Grill 5 to 8 minutes longer or till fish flakes easily when tested with a fork, brushing often with remaining marinade.

(*Or*, to broil fish, place in a greased shallow baking pan. Broil about 4 inches from heat for 6 minutes. Turn fish; baste with some reserved marinade. Broil 2 to 5 minutes more or till fish flakes easily when tested with a fork, brushing often with remaining marinade.)

Makes 2 servings. (Adaptable for one.)†

Baked Halibut Steaks

2 fresh *or* frozen halibut steaks
   or other fish steaks (about
   12 ounces)
4 teaspoons lemon juice
¼ teaspoon salt
⅛ teaspoon paprika
   Dash pepper
2 tablespoons finely chopped
   onion
1 tablespoon butter *or*
   margarine

Thaw fish, if frozen. Combine lemon juice, salt, paprika, and pepper; brush over both sides of fish. Arrange fish steaks in a single layer in a 10×6×2-inch baking dish. Cover and let stand about 30 minutes.

Meanwhile, in small skillet cook onion in butter or margarine till tender but not brown. Spoon cooked onion over fish. Bake in 325° oven for 20 to 25 minutes or till fish flakes easily when tested with a fork. Makes 2 servings. (Adaptable for one.)†

Tartar Sauce

½ cup mayonnaise *or* salad
   dressing
1 tablespoon sweet *or* dill
   pickle relish
1 teaspoon snipped parsley
1 teaspoon chopped pimiento
½ teaspoon grated onion

In small mixing bowl combine mayonnaise or salad dressing, pickle relish, parsley, pimiento, and grated onion. Cover and chill thoroughly. Serve with any cooked hot or cold fish and seafood. Makes ½ cup sauce.

Salmon Loaf

1 7¾-ounce can salmon
1 beaten egg
¾ cup soft bread crumbs
   (1 slice)
1 tablespoon thinly sliced
   green onion
¼ teaspoon salt
⅛ teaspoon pepper
1 tablespoon thinly sliced
   green onion
1 tablespoon butter *or*
   margarine
2 teaspoons all-purpose flour
¼ teaspoon salt
¼ teaspoon dry mustard
   Dash pepper
½ cup milk
½ teaspoon worcestershire
   sauce

Drain salmon, reserving 2 tablespoons liquid. Flake salmon, discarding skin and bones.

In mixing bowl combine the reserved salmon liquid, beaten egg, soft bread crumbs, 1 tablespoon sliced green onion, ¼ teaspoon salt, and ⅛ teaspoon pepper. Add flaked salmon; mix well. Turn salmon mixture into a well-greased 6×3×2-inch loaf pan. Bake in 350° oven about 35 minutes or till done.

For sauce, in small saucepan cook 1 tablespoon sliced green onion in butter or margarine till tender but not brown. Blend in flour, ¼ teaspoon salt, mustard, and dash pepper. Add milk and worcestershire sauce all at once. Cook, stirring constantly, till thickened and bubbly.

Spoon some of the sauce atop salmon loaf; pass the remaining sauce. Makes 2 servings.

Serve crispy Fish and Chips, *the favorite English fish and French fries combo. Try it with a sprinkling of malt vinegar!*

Skillet Fried Fish

2 fresh *or* frozen pan-dressed
   trout *or* other fish (about 6
   ounces each)
2 tablespoons yellow cornmeal
1 tablespoon all-purpose flour
¼ teaspoon salt
⅛ teaspoon paprika
⅛ teaspoon cayenne
3 tablespoons milk
   Cooking oil *or* shortening

Thaw fish, if frozen. Sprinkle cavities generously with salt and pepper. Combine cornmeal, flour, salt, paprika, and cayenne. Dip fish in milk, then coat evenly with cornmeal mixture.

In large skillet heat a small amount of cooking oil or shortening on range top *or* over *hot* coals. Fry fish in hot oil or shortening for 4 to 5 minutes or till lightly browned. Turn and fry 4 to 5 minutes longer or till fish flakes easily when tested with a fork. (Add additional oil or shortening to heated skillet, if needed.) Drain fish on paper toweling. Serve with lemon wedges, if desired. Makes 2 servings. (Adaptable for one.)†

Determine the cooking temperature of coals by holding your hand just above hot coals at the height food will be cooking. Begin counting "one thousand one, one thousand two;" if you need to withdraw your hand after 2 seconds, the coals are **hot,** *3 seconds for* **medium-hot** *coals, 4 seconds for* **medium** *coals, and 5 to 6 seconds for* **slow** *coals.*

†See page 3 for directions.

Fish and Chips

½ pound fresh *or* frozen fish
   fillets
1 large *or* 2 small baking
   potatoes, peeled
2 tablespoons all-purpose
   flour
¼ teaspoon salt
1 tablespoon water
1 teaspoon cooking oil
1 egg yolk
1 stiff-beaten egg white
   Fat for deep-fat frying
2 tablespoons all-purpose
   flour
   Malt vinegar (optional)

Thaw fish, if frozen. Cut fish into 2 serving-size pieces. Pat dry with paper toweling. Cut potatoes lengthwise into ⅜-inch-wide strips.

For batter, in mixing bowl stir together 2 tablespoons flour and ¼ teaspoon salt. Add water, cooking oil, and egg yolk; beat till mixture is smooth. Fold in stiff-beaten egg white.

Fry a few potato strips at a time in deep hot fat (375°) for 5 to 6 minutes or till golden. Remove and drain on paper toweling. Sprinkle with some salt. Cover with foil to keep warm.

Coat fish pieces evenly with 2 tablespoons flour, then dip in batter. Fry in deep hot fat (375°) for 2 to 2½ minutes on each side or till golden. Remove and drain on paper toweling.

To serve, sprinkle fish with a little salt. Drizzle with malt vinegar, if desired. Serve with fried potatoes. Makes 2 servings.

Breaded Fish Portions with Dill Sauce

¼ cup dairy sour cream
1 tablespoon mayonnaise *or* salad dressing
½ teaspoon dried dillweed
2 frozen, fried, breaded fish portions

For sauce, in small mixing bowl combine sour cream, mayonnaise or salad dressing, and dillweed. Cover and chill about 1 hour.

Place fish portions in greased shallow baking pan or in broiler pan. Broil about 4 inches from heat for 5 minutes. Turn fish portions and broil for 5 to 6 minutes.

Spoon the sauce atop broiled fish. Makes 1 serving.

Try these easy coatings for fried fish. Dip 2 fish fillets, steaks, or pan-dressed fish in 2 tablespoons all-purpose flour seasoned with salt and pepper, then in mixture of 1 beaten egg and 1 tablespoon water. Coat fish with one of the following mixtures:
—*Combination of ¼ cup crushed saltine crackers and 1 tablespoon grated parmesan cheese.*
—*Combination of ½ cup instant mashed potato flakes and 1 tablespoon onion salad dressing mix.*

Tuna and Broccoli Casserole for One

½ cup frozen chopped broccoli
1 3¼-ounce can tuna, drained and flaked
¼ cup quick-cooking rice*
¼ cup water
¼ teaspoon salt
   Dash pepper
¼ cup shredded sharp American cheese (1 ounce)

Cook broccoli according to package directions; drain well. In a 12-ounce casserole combine broccoli, tuna, uncooked rice, water, salt, and pepper. Bake, covered, in 350° oven about 25 minutes or till rice is tender. Sprinkle cheese atop. Bake, uncovered, 2 to 3 minutes more or till cheese melts. Makes 1 serving.

Microwave cooking directions: In a 12-ounce nonmetal casserole combine *uncooked* broccoli and 3 tablespoons *water*. Cook, covered with waxed paper, in countertop microwave oven on high power about 2 minutes or till nearly tender; drain.

In a 2-cup glass measure combine the ¼ cup water, salt, and pepper. Micro-cook about 1 minute or till boiling. Stir in uncooked rice*; cover and let stand about 5 minutes or till rice is tender.

Add rice mixture and tuna to broccoli in casserole; mix well. Micro-cook, covered, about 1 minute or till heated through. Sprinkle with cheese; micro-cook, uncovered, about 30 seconds more or till cheese melts.

Use Minute Rice when preparing the casserole in a microwave oven.

Bouillabaisse

1 8-ounce fresh *or* frozen lobster tail
¼ pound fresh *or* frozen fish fillets
4 clams in shells
1 8-ounce can tomatoes, cut up
1 cup water
½ cup dry white wine
1 medium onion, cut up
2 parsley sprigs
1 clove garlic, minced
1 bay leaf
¾ teaspoon salt
¾ teaspoon dried thyme, crushed
¼ teaspoon saffron, crushed
⅛ teaspoon pepper
   French bread

Partially thaw lobster and fish, if frozen. Split lobster tail in half lengthwise, then cut in half crosswise to make 4 portions. Cut fish fillets into 1-inch pieces. Thoroughly wash clams. Cover clams with salted water (3 tablespoons salt to ½ gallon cold water); let stand 15 minutes; rinse. Repeat twice.

In medium saucepan combine tomatoes, water, wine, onion, parsley, garlic, bay leaf, salt, thyme, saffron, and pepper. Simmer, covered, for 30 minutes. Strain the tomato mixture; discard vegetables and herbs.

Bring the strained mixture to boiling; add lobster, fish, and clams. Cook about 5 minutes or till fish flakes easily and clams open. Serve with French bread. Makes 2 servings.

Shrimp and Wine-Sauced Spaghetti

2 tablespoons thinly sliced
   green onion
1 clove garlic, minced
2 teaspoons cooking oil
1 16-ounce can tomatoes, cut
   up
2 tablespoons dry white wine
1 teaspoon sugar
1 teaspoon dried basil,
   crushed
¼ teaspoon salt
¼ teaspoon dried oregano,
   crushed
   Dash pepper
½ pound fresh *or* frozen
   shrimp, shelled
1 tablespoon cornstarch
1 tablespoon cold water
   Hot cooked spaghetti
1 tablespoon grated romano *or*
   parmesan cheese

In small saucepan cook green onion and garlic in hot oil till onion is tender. Add *undrained* tomatoes, white wine, sugar, basil, salt, oregano, and pepper. Cover and simmer for 25 minutes. Add shrimp. Bring to boiling; reduce heat. Simmer, uncovered, about 5 minutes or till shrimp is tender.

Blend cornstarch and water; stir into shrimp mixture. Cook and stir till thickened and bubbly. Serve shrimp mixture over hot cooked spaghetti. Sprinkle with romano or parmesan cheese. Makes 2 servings.

Scallops Tetrazzini

6 to 8 ounces frozen scallops
1 tablespoon chopped onion
¼ teaspoon salt
   Dash pepper
¼ cup water
1 tablespoon butter *or*
   margarine
1 tablespoon all-purpose flour
¼ teaspoon salt
⅛ teaspoon paprika
   Dash dried oregano, crushed
   Dash bottled hot pepper
   sauce
½ cup milk
1 2½-ounce jar sliced
   mushrooms
1 slightly beaten egg
3 ounces spaghetti, cooked
   and drained
1 tablespoon grated parmesan
   cheese

Halve any large scallops. In small saucepan combine scallops, onion, ¼ teaspoon salt, and pepper. Add water. Bring to boiling; reduce heat. Cover and simmer about 3 minutes. Drain, reserving ⅓ cup cooking liquid.

In 1½-quart saucepan melt butter. Blend in flour, ¼ teaspoon salt, paprika, oregano, and hot pepper sauce. Add the reserved ⅓ cup cooking liquid, milk, and *undrained* mushrooms. Cook and stir till thickened and bubbly. Stir about ½ cup of the hot mixture into beaten egg. Return to hot mixture in saucepan. Cook and stir 1 minute longer. Stir in scallops and spaghetti; heat through.

Turn into a 6½×6½×2-inch baking dish. Sprinkle with parmesan cheese. Broil about 4 inches from heat for 2 to 3 minutes or till cheese is lightly browned. Makes 2 servings.

Seafood Medley

1 cup frozen cut green beans
1 7½-ounce can semi-
   condensed cream of
   mushroom with wine soup
¼ cup milk*
1 tablespoon chopped
   pimiento
¼ teaspoon dried thyme,
   crushed
   Dash salt
   Dash cayenne
1 cup cooked rice
1 3¼-ounce can tuna, drained
   and broken into chunks
1 4½-ounce can shrimp,
   drained and deveined
¼ cup canned French-fried
   onions

Cook green beans according to package directions; drain and set aside. In mixing bowl combine mushroom soup, milk, pimiento, thyme, salt, and cayenne. Stir *half* of the soup mixture into cooked rice; fold in tuna.

Turn tuna-rice mixture into a 1-quart casserole. Spread green beans over mixture; top with shrimp. Pour remaining soup mixture over all. Bake, covered, in 350° oven for 25 to 30 minutes or till heated through. Sprinkle with onions. Bake, uncovered, about 5 minutes longer. Makes 2 servings.

For a wine-flavored dish, substitute dry white wine for half the milk.

Retain flavorful juices in Individual Clambakes *by sealing foil packets tightly before grilling.*

Individual Clambakes

8 clams in shells
2 8-ounce frozen lobster tails,
thawed
4 chicken pieces
4 teaspoons butter *or*
margarine, melted
Rockweed *or* parsley sprigs
2 ears fresh corn
6 tablespoons butter *or*
margarine, melted

Thoroughly wash clams. Cover clams with salted water (3 tablespoons salt to ½ gallon cold water); let stand 15 minutes; rinse. Repeat twice. With sharp kitchen scissors, snip along each side of the thin undershell of lobster tails. Remove the undershell. Brush chicken pieces with the 4 teaspoons melted butter. Grill chicken over *hot* coals, skin side down, for 10 minutes.

Meanwhile, tear off four 3-foot lengths of wide heavy foil. Form a package by placing 1 sheet crosswise over another sheet. Repeat, making a second package. Place a handful of rockweed or parsley in center of each package. Cut two 18-inch squares of cheesecloth; place 1 square atop rockweed or parsley in each package. Arrange the following in each package: 4 clams in shells, 1 lobster tail, 2 chicken pieces, and 1 ear of corn. Securely tie opposite ends of cheesecloth around seafood, chicken, and corn. Tightly seal opposite ends of foil.

Place packages on grill, seam side up, over *hot* coals. Grill about 45 minutes or till chicken is done. Divide the 6 tablespoons melted butter or margarine between 2 individual cups. Serve with seafood, chicken, and corn. Makes 2 servings. (Adaptable for one.)†

Clams in Coquilles

1 7½-ounce can minced clams
¼ cup chopped celery
2 tablespoons chopped onion
1 tablespoon butter *or* margarine
2 teaspoons all-purpose flour
½ teaspoon salt
⅛ teaspoon dried thyme, crushed
   Few drops bottled hot pepper sauce
   Dash pepper
¼ cup milk *or* clam liquid
1 beaten egg
½ cup soft bread crumbs
2 teaspoons snipped parsley
2 teaspoons butter *or* margarine, melted
2 tablespoons shredded Swiss cheese

Drain clams; reserve ¼ cup clam liquid, if desired. In small saucepan cook celery and onion in 1 tablespoon butter till tender but not brown. Blend in flour, salt, thyme, hot pepper sauce, and pepper. Add milk *or* the reserved ¼ cup clam liquid. Cook and stir till thickened and bubbly. Stir about half the hot mixture into beaten egg; return to remaining hot mixture in saucepan. Stir in clams, *half* the bread crumbs, and parsley.

Spoon clam mixture into 2 buttered coquilles (individual baking shells) or 6-ounce custard cups. Toss the remaining bread crumbs with 2 teaspoons melted butter; sprinkle over clam mixture. Bake in 400° oven about 10 minutes or till browned. Sprinkle with Swiss cheese. Bake about 1 minute longer or till cheese melts. Makes 2 servings.

Shrimp Curry

1 7½-ounce can semi-condensed cream of mushroom with wine soup
1 teaspoon minced dried onion
1 teaspoon curry powder
½ teaspoon dried parsley flakes
¼ teaspoon paprika
1 7-ounce package (2 cups) frozen shelled shrimp
¼ cup dairy sour cream
   Hot cooked rice
   Assorted condiments: raisins, coarsely chopped peanuts, chutney, chopped tomato, chopped green pepper, *and/or* shredded *or* flaked coconut

In 1-quart saucepan combine mushroom with wine soup, dried onion, curry powder, parsley flakes, and paprika. Bring to boiling, stirring occasionally. Stir in shelled shrimp; return to boiling. Reduce heat; cover and simmer for 5 to 10 minutes or till shrimp is tender.

Gradually stir about ½ cup of the hot mixture into the sour cream; return to remaining hot mixture in saucepan. Heat through but *do not boil*. Spoon curry mixture over hot cooked rice; serve with any of the assorted condiments. Makes 2 servings. (Adaptable for one.)†

Cheese-Crab Rarebit

¼ cup chopped fresh mushrooms
1 tablespoon sliced green onion
1 tablespoon butter *or* margarine
2 teaspoons all-purpose flour
¼ teaspoon dry mustard
¾ cup milk
⅓ cup shredded sharp American cheese
½ teaspoon lemon juice
1 7½-ounce can crab meat, drained, flaked, and cartilage removed
   Toast points *or* toasted English muffin halves

In saucepan cook mushrooms and onion in butter or margarine till tender but not brown. Blend in flour and dry mustard. Add milk all at once. Cook and stir till thickened and bubbly.

Add cheese and lemon juice, stirring till cheese is melted. Fold in crab meat. Heat through. Serve at once over toast points or toasted English muffin halves. Makes 2 servings.

Microwave cooking directions: In 1-quart nonmetal casserole combine mushrooms, onion, and butter. Cook, uncovered, in countertop microwave oven on high power about 2 minutes or till tender. Blend in flour and mustard. Stir in milk. Micro-cook, uncovered, about 2 minutes or till thickened and bubbly; stir every 30 seconds.

Stir in cheese and lemon juice. Micro-cook, uncovered, about 1 minute more or till cheese is melted, stirring once. Fold in crab meat; micro-cook, covered, about 2 minutes more or till heated through. Serve as above.

†See page 3 for directions.

Eggs & Cheeses

Serve Cheese Soufflé directly from the oven. Break apart the puffy mixture, using tines of two forks back to back, and lift out servings with a spoon.

Cheese Soufflé

2 tablespoons butter
2 tablespoons all-purpose
  flour
¼ teaspoon salt
¼ teaspoon dry mustard
  Dash cayenne
½ cup milk
1 cup shredded sharp
  American cheese
2 egg yolks
2 egg whites
  Mushroom Sauce (optional)

In heavy saucepan melt butter; blend in flour, salt, mustard, and cayenne. Add milk all at once. Cook and stir over medium heat till thickened and bubbly. Reduce heat to low; add cheese, stirring to melt. Remove from heat. Beat egg yolks till thick and lemon-colored. Gradually stir in cheese mixture; cool about 5 minutes. Beat egg whites till stiff peaks form. Gradually pour yolk mixture over whites; fold just till distributed. Pour into *ungreased* 3-cup soufflé dish. (For top hat that puffs in the oven, trace circle through mixture 1 inch from edge and 1 inch deep.) Bake in 300° oven 45 to 50 minutes or till knife inserted off-center comes out clean. Serve immediately. Pass Mushroom Sauce, if desired. Makes 2 servings.

Mushroom Sauce: Cook ½ cup sliced fresh *mushrooms* and 2 tablespoons chopped *green onion* in 2 tablespoons *butter* just till tender. Blend ½ cup *light cream* and 2 teaspoons *cornstarch;* stir into mushroom mixture. Stir in ⅓ cup dry *white wine,* 1 tablespoon snipped *parsley,* ¼ teaspoon *salt,* and dash *pepper.* Cook and stir till bubbly.

Quiche Casseroles

2 slices bacon
¼ cup chopped fresh
    mushrooms
¼ cup chopped celery
2 tablespoons chopped onion
2 eggs
¾ cup milk
1 tablespoon all-purpose flour
½ cup shredded Swiss cheese
    Ground nutmeg

Cook bacon till crisp. Drain, reserving 1 tablespoon drippings. Crumble bacon; set aside. Cook mushrooms, celery, and onion in reserved drippings till tender. Beat eggs, milk, and flour. Stir in cooked vegetables, bacon, and cheese. Turn into two 8- to 10-ounce individual casseroles. Sprinkle lightly with nutmeg.

Place casseroles in shallow baking pan on oven rack. Pour boiling water around casseroles in pan to depth of 1 inch. Bake in 325° oven 20 to 25 minutes or till knife inserted off-center comes out clean. Let stand 5 minutes. Makes 2 servings. (Adaptable for one.)†

Cheese Scrambled Eggs

2 eggs
1 tablespoon milk
2 teaspoons butter
1 slice sharp American or
    Swiss cheese, torn
1 tablespoon thinly sliced
    green onion

Beat together eggs, milk, dash *salt*, and dash *pepper*. In small skillet melt butter; add egg mixture. Cook over medium heat, stirring frequently, till eggs begin to set. Sprinkle with cheese. Continue cooking just till eggs are firm and cheese is melted. Sprinkle with green onion. Makes 1 serving.

Curried Eggs

2 tablespoons butter or
    margarine
1 teaspoon curry powder
1 small apple, peeled and
    chopped (about ½ cup)
¼ cup sliced green onion
1 tablespoon all-purpose flour
⅔ cup milk
⅛ teaspoon salt
    Dash pepper
½ cup shredded sharp
    American cheese
    (2 ounces)
3 hard-cooked eggs, quartered
1 2-ounce can mushroom
    stems and pieces, drained
    Hot cooked rice
    Raisins (optional)
    Flaked or shredded coconut
    (optional)
    Chopped peanuts (optional)

In medium saucepan melt butter or margarine; blend in curry powder. Add apple and green onion; cook about 4 minutes or till tender. Blend in flour; add milk, salt, and pepper. Cook, stirring constantly, till thickened and bubbly.

Stir in cheese till melted. Fold in hard-cooked eggs and mushrooms; heat through. Serve over cooked rice. Pass raisins, coconut, and/or peanuts, if desired. Makes 2 servings. (Adaptable for one.)†

Eggs Buckingham

1 tablespoon butter or
    margarine
1 tablespoon all-purpose flour
    Dash pepper
½ cup milk
½ of a 3- or 4-ounce package
    thinly sliced smoked beef,
    snipped
2 teaspoons butter or
    margarine
2 eggs
1 tablespoon milk
    Dash salt
    Dash pepper
    Dash bottled hot pepper
    sauce
2 large rusks, buttered, or 2
    toasted English muffin
    halves
1 teaspoon snipped parsley

In saucepan melt the 1 tablespoon butter or margarine; blend in flour and dash pepper. Add the ½ cup milk. Cook and stir till thickened and bubbly. Stir in snipped smoked beef; cover and keep warm.

Meanwhile, in small skillet melt the 2 teaspoons butter or margarine. In small bowl beat together eggs, 1 tablespoon milk, salt, dash pepper, and hot pepper sauce. Pour egg mixture into skillet. Cook over medium heat, stirring frequently, till eggs are softly set.

Arrange buttered rusks or English muffin halves on individual plates. Spoon cooked egg mixture over rusks or muffins; cover with warm smoked beef mixture. Sprinkle with snipped parsley. Serve immediately. Makes 2 servings. (Adaptable for one.)†

†See page 3 for directions.

Individualized omelets

For **Basic Omelet,** in mixing bowl beat 2 eggs, 1 tablespoon water, ⅛ teaspoon salt, and dash pepper with a fork till blended but not frothy.

In a 6- or 8-inch omelet pan or skillet with flared sides, heat 1 tablespoon butter or margarine till it sizzles and browns slightly. (Use less butter for pan with a non-stick surface.) Lift and tilt pan to coat sides. Add egg mixture and cook slowly. Run spatula around edge, lifting egg to allow uncooked portion to flow underneath. When set but still shiny, remove from heat. Spoon desired filling across center. Fold one third of omelet (portion nearest handle of pan) over center; slide toward outside of pan. Fold outer third over center and slide out onto serving plate. Add accompanying topping. Makes 1 serving.

Russian Omelet

Fill **Basic Omelet** with cubed cooked *potato*. Top with dairy *sour cream* and snipped *chives*.

Cheese-Sauced Omelet

Before preparing **Basic Omelet,** prepare sauce (makes enough for 2 omelets). In small saucepan cook ¾ cup sliced fresh *mushrooms* in 1 tablespoon *butter or margarine* about 4 minutes or till tender. (Or, use one 2-ounce can mushroom stems and pieces, drained; set aside. Melt butter.)

Blend 1 tablespoon all-purpose *flour* and dash *white pepper* into butter. Add ½ cup *milk.* Cook and stir till bubbly. Stir in ½ cup shredded sharp *American cheese* and ½ teaspoon *prepared mustard.* If using canned mushrooms, stir them into sauce. Heat till cheese melts. Keep warm while preparing omelets.

Fill each omelet with ¼ cup sauce. (Or, fill with warmed leftover vegetables or bits of meat, then add sauce.) Top each with half of the remaining sauce; sprinkle with snipped *parsley.*

Garden Omelet
(pictured on the cover)

Before preparing **Basic Omelet,** in small saucepan combine ½ of an 8-ounce can (½ cup) *pizza sauce,* ¼ cup thinly sliced *zucchini,* ¼ cup sliced fresh or canned *mushrooms,* and 2 tablespoons chopped *onion.* Cook till vegetables are crisp-tender. Keep warm while preparing omelet.

Fill omelet with ¼ cup vegetable mixture. Top with remaining mixture; sprinkle with shredded *cheese* (cheddar, Swiss, monterey jack, American, mozzarella, or gruyère), if desired.

Cheese-Sauced Omelet

Breakfast Omelet

Breakfast Omelet

Fill **Basic Omelet** with cooked whole or sliced brown-and-serve *sausage links.*

Top with a little *maple-flavored syrup or honey.* Garnish with sliced *orange wedges,* if desired.

Salad Omelet

Salad Omelet

Fill **Basic Omelet** with sliced *avocado* and sliced *tomato* (peel tomato, if desired).

Top with mixture of ¼ *avocado,* mashed; 1 tablespoon dairy *sour cream;* and 2 drops bottled hot *pepper sauce.* Garnish with chopped *tomato,* if desired.

Fruited Omelet

Fruited Omelet

Fill **Basic Omelet** with about 2 tablespoons dairy *sour cream or yogurt.*

Top with halved *strawberries,* sliced *peaches,* or *blueberries;* sprinkle with *brown sugar.*

Potato Supper Omelet

2 slices bacon
1 large potato, peeled and
 thinly sliced
2 tablespoons sliced green
 onion
 Dash salt
2 beaten eggs
2 tablespoons milk
⅛ teaspoon salt
⅛ teaspoon dried thyme,
 crushed
 Dash pepper
½ cup shredded sharp
 American cheese
 (2 ounces)

In 6-inch skillet cook bacon till crisp. Drain, reserving 1 tablespoon drippings. Crumble bacon and set aside.

In same skillet combine reserved drippings, potato, green onion, and dash salt. Cover tightly; cook over low heat for 15 to 20 minutes or till potato is barely tender, stirring carefully once or twice.

Combine eggs, milk, ⅛ teaspoon salt, thyme, and pepper. Stir in cheese and crumbled bacon. Pour over potato mixture. Cover and continue cooking over very low heat for 5 to 6 minutes or till surface is set but still shiny. With a wide spatula, loosen sides and bottom and transfer omelet to serving plate. Serve at once. Makes 1 serving.

Breakfast or brunch is just the time to enjoy Skillet Huevos Rancheros. *Gently cook the eggs in a not-too-spicy sauce, then serve on tortillas.*

Skillet Huevos Rancheros

2 tablespoons cooking oil
2 or 4 6-inch tortillas
½ cup chopped onion
1 10-ounce can tomatoes and
 green chili peppers
¼ teaspoon salt
¼ teaspoon chili powder
⅛ teaspoon garlic powder
4 eggs
¼ cup shredded monterey
 jack *or* American cheese
 (1 ounce)
 Bottled hot pepper sauce

In medium skillet heat cooking oil. Fry tortillas, one at a time, in hot oil for 20 to 40 seconds on each side or till crisp and golden. Drain on paper toweling. Keep tortillas warm in foil in 250° oven.

In same skillet cook onion in the remaining oil till tender but not brown. Add tomatoes and green chili peppers, salt, chili powder, and garlic powder. Simmer for 5 to 10 minutes or till slightly thickened. Carefully slide each egg into tomato mixture, taking care not to break yolk. Sprinkle eggs with a little salt and pepper. Cover and cook eggs over low heat for 3 to 4 minutes or till desired doneness.

To serve, place eggs and some tomato mixture on warm tortillas. Sprinkle with shredded cheese. Pass hot pepper sauce. Makes 2 servings.

Beer Rarebit Fondue

2 cups shredded sharp
   American cheese
   (8 ounces)
2 teaspoons cornstarch
¼ teaspoon dry mustard
½ teaspoon worcestershire
   sauce
   Dash bottled hot pepper
   sauce
⅓ cup beer
   French bread, cut into
   bite-size pieces, each with
   1 crust

Have cheese at room temperature. Coat cheese with cornstarch and dry mustard. Add worcestershire sauce and bottled hot pepper sauce; mix well.

In a heavy saucepan heat beer. Gradually add cheese mixture, stirring constantly over medium-low heat, till cheese is melted.

Quickly transfer cheese mixture to fondue pot; keep warm over fondue burner. Spear a bread cube with fondue fork, piercing the crust last. Dip bread into cheese mixture and swirl to coat. The swirling is important to keep the mixture in motion so it doesn't set up.

If mixture thickens while standing, stir in additional beer. Makes 2 servings.

Macaroni and Cheese

½ cup elbow macaroni
2 tablespoons butter or
   margarine
2 tablespoons crushed rich
   round crackers (3 crackers)
2 tablespoons chopped onion
1 tablespoon all-purpose flour
⅛ teaspoon salt
   Dash pepper
1 cup milk
¼ teaspoon worcestershire
   sauce
¾ to 1 cup shredded cheese
   (3 to 4 ounces)*
1 tablespoon chopped
   pimiento

Cook macaroni in boiling salted water about 8 minutes or till just tender. Drain; set aside.

In saucepan melt butter or margarine. Remove 1 tablespoon of the melted butter and toss with cracker crumbs; set aside. Cook onion in the remaining melted butter till tender but not brown. Blend in flour, salt, and pepper. Add milk and worcestershire sauce; cook and stir till mixture is thickened and bubbly.

Stir in cheese till melted. Stir in pimiento and cooked macaroni. Turn mixture into two 10-ounce casseroles; sprinkle with cracker crumb mixture. Bake in 350° oven for 15 to 20 minutes. Makes 2 servings. (Adaptable for one.)†

Try any of your favorite cheeses, using the smaller amount if you prefer a mild flavor. Process cheeses, such as American, process Swiss, gruyère, or monterey jack give a smoother texture than natural cheeses.

Herb-Sauced Fettucini

3 ounces fettucini or medium
   noodles (about 2 cups)
1 3-ounce package cream
   cheese, softened
¼ cup milk
1 tablespoon snipped parsley
½ teaspoon dried thyme,
   crushed
⅛ teaspoon pepper
¼ cup grated romano or
   parmesan cheese

Cook fettucini or noodles in a large amount of boiling salted water about 8 minutes or till just tender; drain.

Meanwhile, in small saucepan stir together softened cream cheese, milk, snipped parsley, thyme, and pepper till smooth. Heat cream cheese mixture over low heat just till warm.

Sprinkle cooked fettucini or noodles with *3 tablespoons* of the grated romano or parmesan cheese; toss well to coat fettucini or noodles.

To serve, place fettucini mixture on warm dinner plates. Spoon warm cream cheese mixture over each serving. Sprinkle with the remaining romano or parmesan cheese. Makes 2 servings. (Adaptable for one.)†

†See page 3 for directions.

Main Meal Salads

Chef's Salad

2 cups torn mixed salad
  greens
¾ cup fully cooked ham *or*
  cooked beef cut into thin
  strips
1 small carrot, shredded
¼ cup sliced cucumber
2 ounces Swiss cheese, cut
  into strips
2 tablespoons crumbled blue
  cheese
1 hard-cooked egg, cut into
  wedges
¼ cup salad oil
2 tablespoons wine vinegar
2 tablespoons chili sauce
1 tablespoon snipped parsley
1 tablespoon finely chopped
  onion
¼ teaspoon salt
⅛ teaspoon garlic powder
  Dash pepper

Place salad greens in 2 individual salad bowls. Arrange ham or beef strips, shredded carrot, cucumber, Swiss cheese, blue cheese, and hard-cooked egg atop greens in each salad bowl.

For dressing, in screw-top jar combine salad oil, wine vinegar, chili sauce, parsley, onion, salt, garlic powder, and pepper. Cover and shake well. Pour dressing over salads. Makes 2 servings. (Adaptable for one.)†

Garden Pasta Salad

½ cup salami, pepperoni,
  cervelat, *or* mortadella cut
  into small pieces
1 medium tomato, peeled
  and chopped
¼ cup chopped cucumber
¼ cup chopped green pepper
1 slice medium onion, finely
  chopped
1 tablespoon snipped parsley
  Fresh Herb Dressing
3 ounces spaghetti *or* fettucini,
  broken
¼ cup crumbled feta cheese
  (1 ounce)

In mixing bowl combine sausage, tomato, cucumber, green pepper, onion, and parsley. Toss with Fresh Herb Dressing. Cover and chill thoroughly.

Cook spaghetti or fettucini in a large amount of boiling salted water about 8 minutes or till just tender. Drain; rinse with cold water, then drain again. Continue rinsing and draining till pasta is well chilled.

Turn cooked pasta into a salad bowl. Spoon meat-dressing mixture atop pasta. Sprinkle with crumbled feta cheese. Toss. Makes 2 servings. (Adaptable for one.)†

Fresh Herb Dressing: In screw-top jar combine ¼ cup *salad oil;* 3 tablespoons dry *white wine;* 2 tablespoons *lemon juice;* 1 tablespoon *sugar;* 2 teaspoons snipped *fresh basil or* ½ teaspoon *dried basil,* crushed; ¼ teaspoon *salt;* ⅛ teaspoon freshly ground *pepper;* and several dashes bottled *hot pepper sauce.* Cover and shake well.

†See page 3 for directions.

Either spaghetti or fettucini forms the base for sausage, vegetables, cheese, and an herb-wine dressing in Garden Pasta Salad.

Taco Salad

½ pound ground beef
1 8-ounce can tomatoes
2 cups torn lettuce
½ cup shredded sharp
   American *or* cheddar
   cheese
¼ cup sliced green onion
6 pitted ripe olives, sliced
1 3⅛-ounce can (about ⅓ cup)
   jalapeño bean dip
1 teaspoon chili powder
¼ teaspoon salt
½ cup corn chips

In skillet brown meat; drain off fat. Drain tomatoes, reserving liquid. Cut up tomatoes. In salad bowl combine lettuce, cheese, onion, olives, and tomatoes.

To meat in skillet, stir in reserved tomato liquid, bean dip, chili powder, and salt; bring to boiling. Add to lettuce mixture; toss well. Top with chips. Serve at once. Makes 2 servings.

Tuna Salad Plate

1 3¼-ounce can tuna, drained
   and broken into chunks
½ cup chopped apple
1 tablespoon chopped green
   onion
3 tablespoons mayonnaise
1 teaspoon lemon juice
⅛ teaspoon salt
   Dash pepper
   Lettuce leaves
1 medium tomato, cut into 6
   wedges

Combine tuna, apple, and onion. Combine mayonnaise, lemon juice, salt, and pepper. Add to tuna mixture; toss lightly. Cover and chill, if desired. Line salad plate with lettuce. Spoon tuna mixture in center of plate. Arrange tomato around tuna mixture. Makes 1 serving.

Dilled Salmon-Macaroni Salad

½ cup elbow macaroni
¼ cup chopped cucumber
2 tablespoons chopped green
   pepper
2 tablespoons sliced green
   onion
⅓ cup mayonnaise *or* salad
   dressing
½ teaspoon dried dillweed
¼ teaspoon salt
⅛ teaspoon pepper
1 7¾-ounce can salmon,
   drained and slightly
   flaked
   Lettuce leaves
1 hard-cooked egg, cut into 8
   wedges

Cook macaroni in boiling salted water about 8 minutes or just till tender; drain well.

In mixing bowl combine cooked macaroni, cucumber, green pepper, and green onion. Stir in mayonnaise or salad dressing, dillweed, salt, and pepper; mix thoroughly. Fold in salmon. Season to taste with additional salt. Cover and chill at least 2 hours.

Spoon salmon mixture into 2 individual lettuce-lined salad bowls. Arrange hard-cooked egg wedges atop each salad. Makes 2 servings. (Adaptable for one.)†

Shrimp and Crab with Louis Dressing

¼ cup dairy sour cream
2 tablespoons mayonnaise *or* salad dressing
2 tablespoons chili sauce
1 tablespoon chopped green pepper
1 tablespoon chopped onion
1 teaspoon lemon juice
½ teaspoon prepared horseradish
¼ teaspoon prepared mustard
¼ teaspoon worcestershire sauce
 Dash salt
 Dash pepper
 Dash paprika
1½ cups fresh *or* frozen shelled medium shrimp, cooked and chilled
1 6-ounce package frozen crab meat, cooked and chilled
2 lettuce cups
2 tablespoons sliced pitted ripe olives
1 tablespoon snipped parsley
2 lemon wedges

For dressing, in small mixing bowl combine sour cream, mayonnaise or salad dressing, chili sauce, green pepper, onion, lemon juice, horseradish, mustard, worcestershire sauce, salt, pepper, and paprika. Cover and chill thoroughly.

Just before serving, arrange chilled shrimp and crab meat in lettuce cups. Spoon dressing over each salad. Garnish with sliced olives and snipped parsley; arrange lemon wedges on the side. Makes 2 servings.

Marinated Shrimp Luncheon Salad

1 7-ounce package (2 cups) frozen shelled shrimp
1 small pineapple
⅓ cup coarsely chopped celery
⅓ cup sliced fresh mushrooms
¼ cup salad oil
2 tablespoons dry white wine
1 tablespoon honey
⅛ teaspoon salt

In saucepan cook shrimp in boiling salted water according to package directions; drain and cool. Halve the pineapple lengthwise, leaving leaves with each portion. Cut out the fruit, leaving a ½-inch-thick shell. Remove and discard the hard inner core; cut fruit into chunks. Cover pineapple shells and refrigerate.

In mixing bowl combine pineapple chunks, cooked shrimp, celery, and mushrooms; toss together lightly.

For marinade, in screw-top jar combine salad oil, wine, honey, and salt. Cover and shake well. Pour over pineapple-shrimp mixture; stir to coat well. Cover and refrigerate for 2 to 4 hours, stirring occasionally.

Just before serving, spoon the pineapple-marinade mixture into chilled pineapple shells. Makes 2 servings. (Adaptable for one.)†

Avocado-Chicken Salad Amandine

1 whole medium chicken breast
1 small bay leaf
2 tablespoons French salad dressing
1 teaspoon lemon juice
¼ teaspoon salt
¼ teaspoon dry mustard
⅛ teaspoon pepper
1 small avocado
¼ cup chopped celery
¼ cup mayonnaise *or* salad dressing
1 tablespoon chopped pimiento
2 teaspoons drained capers (optional)
 Lettuce leaves
1 tablespoon toasted slivered almonds
1 tablespoon snipped parsley

Cook chicken breast with bay leaf in boiling salted water about 20 minutes or till tender. Cool thoroughly in the broth. Remove chicken breast; discard skin and bones. Coarsely chop the meat. (Reserve the chicken broth for another use.)

In mixing bowl combine French salad dressing, lemon juice, salt, mustard, and pepper. Add chopped chicken and toss lightly. Chill well.

Before serving, seed and peel avocado; cut fruit into cubes (should measure about ¾ cup). Add avocado, celery, mayonnaise or salad dressing, pimiento, and capers to chicken mixture; mix well. Spoon into individual lettuce-lined salad bowls. Sprinkle each salad with toasted slivered almonds and snipped parsley. Makes 2 servings.

†See page 3 for directions.

Soups & Sandwiches

Homemade Chicken Noodle Soup

½ medium chicken breast
  (about 4 ounces)
 2 cups water
¼ cup chopped onion
 1 small bay leaf
½ teaspoon salt
  Dash pepper
 1 medium ear fresh corn
¼ cup medium noodles
¼ cup chopped celery
 2 tablespoons snipped parsley

In 2-quart saucepan combine chicken breast, water, onion, bay leaf, salt, and pepper. Bring to boiling; reduce heat. Simmer, covered, for 15 to 20 minutes or till chicken is tender.

Meanwhile, with sharp knife make cuts through center of corn kernels in each row of the ear. Cut corn off cob; scrape cob.

Remove chicken from broth; cool slightly. Discard skin and bones; cut up meat (should measure about ½ cup). Set meat aside. Skim fat from broth. Discard bay leaf. Bring broth to boiling. Add corn, noodles, celery, and parsley to hot broth. Simmer, covered, about 8 minutes or till corn and noodles are tender. Add chicken; heat through. Season to taste with salt and pepper. Makes 2 servings.

Spanish Hamburger Soup

¼ pound ground beef
 1 8-ounce can tomato sauce
 1 medium carrot, sliced
 1 2-ounce can mushroom
   stems and pieces
 2 tablespoons chopped onion
 2 tablespoons sliced
   pimiento-stuffed olives
½ teaspoon sugar
½ cup water
¼ cup dry red wine

In saucepan cook beef browned; drain fat. Sprinkle w ¼ teaspoon *salt* and dash *pe per*. Add tomato sauce, carr mushrooms, onion, olives, a sugar. Stir in water and wir Cover; simmer for 30 to 35 m utes or till carrot is tender, stirri occasionally. Sprinkle individu servings with a little grated p mesan cheese, if desired. Mak 2 servings.

Clam Chowder

½ cup shredded American
   cheese (2 ounces)
 1 teaspoon cornstarch*
 1 7½-ounce can minced clam
⅔ cup milk
¼ teaspoon worcestershire
   sauce
  Dash garlic powder
 1 8-ounce can tomatoes, cut
 2 slices French bread, toaste
 1 teaspoon snipped parsley

Toss cheese with cornstarch. small saucepan combine chee mixture, *undrained* clams, m worcestershire, and garlic po der. Add *undrained* tomato Cook and stir till thickened a bubbly. Ladle into 2 bowls; t with toasted bread. Sprinkle w parsley. Makes 2 servings.

Double the amount of co starch for a thick chowder.

Sit down to hearty Spanish Hamburger Soup. It's packed full of beef, carr and mushrooms and simmered in a tangy tomato sauce.

Tuna Chowder

2 tablespoons sliced green
    onion
1 tablespoon butter
1 10¾-ounce can condensed
    cream of potato soup
⅔ cup milk
2 tablespoons dry white wine
½ teaspoon worcestershire
    sauce
⅛ teaspoon pepper
1 6½- or 7-ounce can tuna,
    drained and broken into
    chunks

In saucepan cook onion in butter till tender. Add soup. Gradually stir in milk, wine, worcestershire, and pepper. Add tuna; heat through. Makes 2 servings.
Microwave cooking directions: In 1-quart nonmetal casserole combine onion and butter. Cook, uncovered, in countertop microwave oven on high power about 2 minutes or till tender. Stir in next 5 ingredients; add tuna. Micro-cook, uncovered, 7 to 8 minutes; stir every 2 minutes.

Sherried Onion Soup

1 medium onion, thinly sliced
1 tablespoon butter
1 10½-ounce can condensed
    beef broth
2 tablespoons dry sherry
2 ½-inch-thick slices French
    bread, toasted
¼ cup shredded Swiss or
    grated parmesan cheese

Cook onion in butter about 10 minutes or till tender. Add broth and sherry; bring to boiling. Sprinkle toast slices with cheese; place under broiler till cheese is lightly browned. Ladle soup into 2 bowls; float toast slices atop. Makes 2 servings. (Adaptable for one.)†

Herbed Tomato Soup

1 small onion, thinly sliced
    (¼ cup)
1 tablespoon butter or
    margarine
1 teaspoon all-purpose flour
2 medium tomatoes, peeled
    and quartered, or 1
    8-ounce can tomatoes
2 teaspoons snipped fresh
    basil or ½ teaspoon dried
    basil, crushed
1 teaspoon instant chicken
    bouillon granules
1 teaspoon snipped fresh
    thyme or ¼ teaspoon dried
    thyme, crushed
¼ teaspoon salt
    Dash pepper
1 cup water
    Dairy sour cream (optional)

In 1-quart saucepan cook onion in butter till tender but not brown. Blend in flour. Stir in fresh or canned tomatoes, basil, chicken bouillon granules, thyme, salt, and pepper; mash tomatoes slightly. Stir in water; bring tomato mixture to boiling. Reduce heat; cover and simmer for 30 minutes.

Place hot tomato mixture in blender container. Cover and blend till pureed. Strain. Return strained tomato mixture to saucepan; heat through. Ladle into soup bowl. Garnish with dollop of dairy sour cream, if desired. Makes 1 serving.

Steak Sandwiches with Mushrooms

2 beef cubed steaks
1 tablespoon butter
⅛ teaspoon salt
    Dash pepper
2 slices Swiss cheese
2 slices French or vienna
    bread, toasted and
    buttered
1 2½-ounce jar sliced
    mushrooms, drained
1 tablespoon sliced green
    onion
2 tablespoons dry red wine

In 8-inch skillet quickly brown steaks on both sides in butter. Season with salt and pepper. Place cheese slice atop each steak; cover pan about 1 minute or till cheese melts. Place steaks on toasted bread; keep warm.

Blend mushrooms, onion, and wine into pan drippings; heat through. Pour over steak sandwiches. Makes 2 sandwiches. (Adaptable for one.)†

Super Sausage Sandwiches

3 fully cooked smoked
    sausage links, halved
    lengthwise
1 cup shredded cabbage
3 tablespoons dry red wine
½ teaspoon minced dried onion
⅛ teaspoon celery seed
    Prepared mustard
2 French rolls, split and
    warmed

In 8-inch skillet combine sausages and cabbage; stir in wine, onion, and celery seed. Cover; simmer about 5 minutes. Spread mustard on warm rolls. Lift sausages and cabbage from liquid; spoon onto rolls. Spoon a little wine mixture over sausages and cabbage. Makes 2 sandwiches.

Garden-Fresh Subs, *layered with vegetables, cheese, and salami and accented with an herb spread, is a new way to satisfy an old-fashioned appetite.*

Garden-Fresh Subs

½ cup dairy sour cream
1 teaspoon dried mixed salad
    herbs
⅛ teaspoon garlic salt
2 individual French rolls, split
2 lettuce leaves
2 slices salami
2 slices sharp American
    cheese
1 slice Swiss cheese, halved
    crosswise
1 small tomato, peeled and
    sliced
½ small cucumber, thinly
    sliced (½ cup)
½ small green pepper, sliced
    crosswise into rings
¼ cup sliced pitted ripe olives
2 tablespoons sliced green
    onion

For herb spread, in small mixing bowl combine dairy sour cream, mixed salad herbs, and the garlic salt. Cover and chill thoroughly.

Spread cut surfaces of rolls with chilled herb spread. On bottom half of each roll arrange lettuce, salami, American cheese, Swiss cheese, and tomato. Top each with cucumber, green pepper, olives, and green onion. Place top half of roll over filling, anchoring with wooden picks, if needed. Makes 2 sandwiches. (Adaptable for one.)†

Grilled Ham and Cheese Deluxe

2 slices rye bread
    Dijon-style mustard
2 slices boiled ham
1 slice salami
2 or 3 thin slices tomato
1 slice Swiss cheese
    Butter *or* margarine, softened

Spread rye bread slices with a little dijon-style mustard. Top 1 of the slices with ham, salami, tomato, then cheese. Top with remaining bread slice, mustard side down.

Spread top and bottom of sandwich with softened butter or margarine. Cook in skillet or on griddle on both sides, over medium heat, till sandwich is heated through and cheese is melted. Makes 1 sandwich.

Broiled Bacon-Tomato Muffins

2 slices bacon, cut in half
    crosswise
2 tablespoons chopped onion
2 English muffin halves,
    toasted
2 slices tomato
1 slice American cheese, cut
    diagonally into quarters

In skillet cook bacon till crisp; drain, reserving 1 tablespoon drippings. Cook onion in reserved drippings till tender.

Place muffin halves on baking sheet. Top each with cooked onion and tomato. Broil 4 to 5 inches from heat about 2 minutes or till tomato is heated through. Top each with bacon pieces, then cheese triangles. Broil about 1 minute longer or till cheese just melts. Makes 1 serving.

†See page 3 for directions.

SIDE DISHES
SALADS

Stuffed Zucchini
(see recipe, page 68)

Sesame Salad Toss

Sesame Salad Toss

3 tablespoons salad oil
¼ teaspoon finely shredded lime peel
1 tablespoon lime juice
1½ teaspoons sesame seed, toasted
1 teaspoon sugar
⅛ teaspoon dry mustard
Dash salt
1½ cups torn fresh spinach *or* leaf lettuce
1 small peach, peeled, pitted, and sliced, *or* 1 small nectarine, pitted and sliced
½ avocado, seeded, peeled, and sliced
4 cherry tomatoes, halved

For dressing, in small screw-top jar combine first 7 ingredients. Cover; shake well. Chill.

In salad bowl combine spinach, peach, avocado, and tomatoes. Shake dressing and toss with salad. Makes 2 servings.

Wilted Spinach Salad

4 cups fresh spinach
2 tablespoons sliced green onion
Dash freshly ground pepper
2 slices bacon
2 tablespoons vinegar
1 teaspoon sugar
1 teaspoon dijon-style mustard
¼ teaspoon dried tarragon, crushed
⅛ teaspoon salt

Wash spinach; pat dry on paper toweling. Tear into a bowl. Add onion; sprinkle with pepper. Chill. Cut bacon into small pieces. In skillet cook bacon till crisp. Blend in vinegar, sugar, mustard, tarragon, and salt. Gradually add spinach and green onion, tossing just till spinach is coated and slightly wilted. Serve on 2 large salad plates. Makes 2 servings. (Adaptable for one.)†

†See page 3 for directions.

Try any of these easy salad ideas to create an appetizing, colorful, and quick-to-fix menu addition.

—*Top pear half with shredded American or cheddar cheese.*

—*Serve slices of tomato and onion with your favorite salad dressing.*

—*Enhance tossed salads by adding chopped hard-cooked egg, mandarin orange sections, raw vegetables such as cauliflower, sliced olives, crumbled crisp-cooked bacon, shredded cheese or cheese cubes, and/or seasoned croutons.*

—*Combine equal amounts whipped cream and sweet French salad dressing. Serve mixture over fresh or canned fruit.*

Tomato-Zucchini Salad

1 tablespoon mayonnaise *or* salad dressing
1 tablespoon French salad dressing
1 teaspoon wheat germ
¼ teaspoon sugar
¼ teaspoon vinegar
1 cup torn lettuce
½ small tomato, cut into wedges
¼ cup thinly sliced zucchini

Combine mayonnaise, French salad dressing, wheat germ, sugar, and vinegar. Place lettuce in individual salad bowl; top with tomato wedges and zucchini. Pour dressing mixture atop; toss lightly. Makes 1 serving.

Cucumbers in Sour Cream

1 small cucumber
½ small onion, thinly sliced and separated into rings
¼ cup vinegar
1 teaspoon sugar
¼ cup dairy sour cream
¼ teaspoon dillseed
Dash bottled hot pepper sauce

Thinly slice cucumber (should measure about 1¼ cups). Combine cucumber and onion; sprinkle with ½ teaspoon *salt*. Combine vinegar, sugar, and ¼ cup *water;* pour over cucumber mixture. Let stand at room temperature about 1 hour; drain well. Combine sour cream, dillseed, pepper sauce, and dash *pepper.* Toss with cucumber mixture. Cover; chill at least 1 hour. Makes 2 servings. (Adaptable for one.)†

Creamy Potato Salad

2 small potatoes
¼ cup chopped celery
2 tablespoons thinly sliced green onion
1 hard-cooked egg, coarsely chopped
¼ teaspoon salt
¼ teaspoon celery seed
¼ cup mayonnaise *or* salad dressing
2 teaspoons vinegar
1 teaspoon sugar
1 teaspoon prepared mustard

In covered pan cook potatoes in boiling salted water 20 to 25 minutes or till tender; drain. Peel and cube. Combine potatoes, celery, green onion, egg, salt, celery seed, and dash *pepper.* Combine mayonnaise, vinegar, sugar, and mustard; toss with potato mixture. Chill. Makes 2 servings. (Adaptable for one.)†

Make individual Orange Salad Molds *accented with sour cream dressing a refreshing accompaniment to any meal.*

Orange Salad Molds

½ of a 3-ounce package (3½ tablespoons) orange-flavored gelatin
¾ cup boiling water
¼ cup finely chopped unpeeled apple
2 tablespoons finely chopped walnuts
¼ cup dairy sour cream
1 teaspoon sugar
Lettuce leaves
Finely shredded orange peel (optional)

In mixing bowl dissolve gelatin in boiling water; chill till partially set (consistency of unbeaten egg whites). Fold in chopped apple and walnuts. Pour gelatin mixture into two ½-cup molds. Chill till firm.

Combine sour cream and sugar; chill. Unmold gelatin onto 2 individual lettuce-lined salad plates. Spoon sour cream mixture atop gelatin. Garnish with shredded orange peel, if desired. Makes 2 servings.

Sweet-Sour Coleslaw

1½ cups finely shredded green *or* red cabbage
1 tablespoon finely chopped onion
2 tablespoons mayonnaise *or* salad dressing
1 tablespoon sweet pickle relish
2 teaspoons sugar
2 teaspoons vinegar
¼ teaspoon salt
¼ teaspoon celery seed

In bowl combine the shredded cabbage and onion. Chill.

For dressing combine mayonnaise or salad dressing, pickle relish, sugar, vinegar, salt, and celery seed, stirring till sugar is completely dissolved. Chill. To serve, pour the dressing over the cabbage mixture; toss lightly to coat. Makes 2 servings. (Adaptable for one.)†

Orange-Beet Salad

¼ cup salad oil
3 tablespoons red wine vinegar
½ teaspoon sugar
⅛ teaspoon salt
⅛ teaspoon dried basil, crushed
Dash pepper
1 8-ounce can sliced beets, chilled
½ small onion, thinly sliced and separated into rings
Leaf *or* bibb lettuce
1 orange, peeled and sectioned

For dressing, in screw-top jar combine salad oil, red wine vinegar, sugar, salt, basil, and pepper. Cover and shake well. Chill till ready to serve.

Drain beets; arrange beets and onion rings on 2 individual lettuce-lined salad plates. Arrange orange sections atop beets and onion rings. Shake dressing; pour desired amount over salads. Makes 2 servings.

Berry-Fruit Salad

⅓ cup pineapple yogurt
2 tablespoons orange juice
2 teaspoons sugar
Dash ground cinnamon
½ cantaloupe, seeded and cut into 2 wedges
Lettuce leaves
1 grapefruit, peeled and sectioned
¼ cup fresh blueberries

For dressing combine the first 4 ingredients. Separate melon from shell; cut into bite-size pieces, leaving pieces in shell. Place on 2 individual lettuce-lined salad plates. Arrange grapefruit and blueberries atop melon. Spoon dressing over fruit. Serves 2.

†See page 3 for directions.

Vegetables

Stuffed Zucchini
(pictured on page 64)

1 zucchini (6 to 7 inches long)
¼ cup water
1 tablespoon butter *or* margarine
¼ cup soft bread crumbs
2 tablespoons chopped pimiento-stuffed olives
2 tablespoons shredded sharp American cheese
Parsley sprigs (optional)

Halve zucchini lengthwise. Scoop out pulp, leaving ¼-inch shell. Chop zucchini pulp (should measure about ⅓ cup); set aside. Place zucchini shells, cut side down, in 8-inch skillet. Add water. Cover and simmer for 5 to 6 minutes or till just tender. Drain. Turn shells, cut side up, in same skillet. Sprinkle with a little salt.

Meanwhile, in small saucepan cook chopped zucchini pulp in butter or margarine about 3 minutes or till squash is tender. Add bread crumbs and olives; toss to combine. Spoon bread crumb mixture into zucchini shells. Top with cheese. Cover and heat for 2 to 3 minutes or till cheese is melted. Garnish with parsley sprigs, if desired. Makes 2 servings. (Adaptable for one.)†

Anise Carrots

3 medium carrots
1 teaspoon granulated *or* brown sugar
½ teaspoon cornstarch
⅛ teaspoon aniseed, crushed
Dash salt
3 tablespoons orange juice
2 teaspoons butter *or* margarine
Parsley sprigs (optional)
Orange twist (optional)

Bias-slice carrots crosswise about ⅛ inch thick (should measure about 1½ cups). In covered saucepan cook carrots in small amount of boiling salted water about 8 minutes or till just tender; drain.

Meanwhile, in small saucepan combine sugar, cornstarch, aniseed, and salt. Stir in orange juice; cook and stir till thickened and bubbly. Remove from heat; stir in butter or margarine. Pour over carrots, tossing to coat evenly. Turn into serving bowl. Garnish with parsley sprigs and orange twist, if desired. Makes 2 servings.

Microwave cooking directions: Bias-slice carrots crosswise about ⅛ inch thick. In a 1-quart nonmetal casserole, combine carrots and ¼ cup *water.* Cook, covered with waxed paper, in countertop microwave oven on high power for 6 to 7 minutes or till just tender; drain.

In 1-cup glass measure combine sugar, cornstarch, aniseed, and salt. Stir in orange juice. Micro-cook, uncovered, for 30 seconds; stir. Micro-cook, uncovered, about 30 seconds longer. Stir in butter or margarine. Pour over carrots, tossing to coat evenly. Season to taste with salt. Serve as above.

Treat broccoli in an extra-special way—serve Curry Cheese-Sauced Broccoli.

Curry Cheese-Sauced Broccoli

½ pound fresh broccoli *or* 1
   10-ounce package frozen
   broccoli spears
1 tablespoon butter *or*
   margarine
1 tablespoon all-purpose flour
¼ teaspoon curry powder*
½ cup milk
¼ cup shredded American
   cheese
¼ cup shredded process Swiss
   cheese

Cut fresh broccoli stalks lengthwise into uniform spears, following the branching lines. In covered saucepan cook fresh broccoli spears in 1 inch of boiling salted water for 10 to 15 minutes or till crisp-tender. (Or, cook frozen broccoli spears according to package directions.) Drain well. Meanwhile, in small saucepan melt butter or margarine; blend in flour, curry powder, and dash *salt*. Add milk all at once. Cook, stirring constantly, till thickened and bubbly. Stir in American and Swiss cheese. Cook, stirring constantly, till cheeses are melted and mixture is smooth. Spoon curry-cheese mixture over broccoli. Makes 2 servings. (Adaptable for one.)†

Add a little more curry powder for a spicier sauce.

†See page 3 for directions.

Cheesy Twice-Baked Potatoes

2 medium baking potatoes
¼ cup dairy sour cream
¼ cup shredded sharp
    American cheese
2 tablespoons thinly sliced
    green onion
2 tablespoons milk
¼ teaspoon salt
    Dash pepper
    Paprika
2 teaspoons grated parmesan
    cheese
1 teaspoon snipped green
    onion tops

Scrub potatoes thoroughly; prick skins. Bake in 425° oven for 45 to 60 minutes or till tender. Cut lengthwise slice from top of each potato; discard skin from slice. Reserving potato shells, scoop out the insides and add to potato portions from top slices; mash. Add sour cream, American cheese, sliced green onion, milk, salt, and pepper. Beat with electric mixer till smooth. Spoon into shells; sprinkle with paprika.

Place in 8×8×2-inch baking pan. Bake, covered, in 350° oven for 20 to 25 minutes or till heated through. Sprinkle with parmesan cheese and onion tops. Bake, uncovered, about 5 minutes. Makes 2 servings. (Adaptable for one.)†

Choose a variety of potato best suited to your particular use. In general, long, oval potatoes have mealy interiors that are best for baking, frying, or mashing. Round potatoes usually have firm, waxy interiors and are best for boiling.

Store potatoes in a cool (about 55°F.), dark place.

Potato Nests with Dilled Peas

Packaged instant mashed
    potatoes (enough for 2
    servings)
1 slightly beaten egg yolk
¼ cup shredded cheddar
    cheese (1 ounce)
1 8½-ounce can peas
    Dried dillweed
2 teaspoons butter

Prepare potatoes according to package directions. Combine potatoes and egg yolk; stir in cheese. Spoon in 2 mounds onto greased baking sheet. Using back of spoon, shape into 2 nests. Drain peas; spoon into nests. Sprinkle with dill; dot with butter. Bake in 325° oven for 40 to 45 minutes. Makes 2 servings.

Apple-Bean Bake

1 16-ounce can pork and beans
    in tomato sauce
1 small apple, peeled, cored,
    and sliced
¼ cup chopped onion
1 tablespoon brown sugar
1 tablespoon light molasses
1 teaspoon prepared mustard

In 5×5×2-inch baking dish combine beans, apple, onion, brown sugar, molasses, and mustard. Bake in 350° oven for 1 to 1½ hours, stirring several times. Let stand a few minutes before serving. Makes 2 servings.

Microwave cooking directions: In a 1-quart nonmetal casserole, combine apple, onion, and ¼ cup *water.* Cook, covered with waxed paper, in countertop microwave oven on high power about 2 minutes or till crisp-tender; drain.

Stir in beans, sugar, molasses, and mustard. Micro-cook, uncovered, for 5 to 6 minutes or till bubbly, stirring twice.

Saucy Brussels Sprouts

1 10-ounce package frozen brussels sprouts
1 tablespoon finely chopped onion
1 tablespoon butter *or* margarine
2 teaspoons brown sugar
1 teaspoon all-purpose flour
¼ teaspoon salt
¼ teaspoon dry mustard
  Dash pepper
¼ cup milk
½ cup dairy sour cream
1 tablespoon chopped pimiento

In saucepan cook brussels sprouts according to package directions; drain. Halve sprouts; set aside. In same saucepan cook onion in butter or margarine till tender but not brown. Blend in brown sugar, flour, salt, mustard, and pepper. Add milk. Cook, stirring constantly, till thickened and bubbly.

Gradually blend about ¼ cup of the hot mixture into sour cream. Return to hot mixture. Add pimiento and brussels sprouts; stir gently to combine. Cook till heated through; *do not boil*. Makes 2 servings. (Adaptable for one.)†

Green Beans Amandine

½ cup frozen French-style green beans
2 teaspoons slivered almonds
1 teaspoon butter *or* margarine
¼ teaspoon lemon juice

Cook green beans according to package directions; drain.

Meanwhile, cook slivered almonds in butter or margarine over low heat till golden, stirring occasionally. Remove from heat; stir in lemon juice. Pour butter mixture over cooked beans. Toss lightly till beans are coated. Makes 1 serving.

Italian Bean Succotash

1 cup frozen Italian green beans
½ cup frozen whole kernel corn
2 tablespoons coarsely chopped onion
2 tablespoons coarsely chopped green pepper
½ cup water
1 tablespoon chopped pimiento (optional)
1 teaspoon butter *or* margarine
½ teaspoon dried dillweed
¼ teaspoon salt
  Dash pepper

In 1½-quart saucepan combine green beans, corn, onion, and green pepper; add water. Bring to boiling; reduce heat. Cover and simmer about 5 minutes or till tender. Drain.

Stir pimiento, butter or margarine, dillweed, salt, and pepper into cooked vegetables. Heat through. Makes 2 servings. (Adaptable for one.)†

Scalloped Swiss Corn

1 beaten egg
1 8-ounce can cream-style corn
½ cup shredded Swiss cheese (2 ounces)
½ cup finely crushed saltine crackers (14 crackers)
3 tablespoons milk
1 tablespoon finely chopped onion
  Dash pepper
2 teaspoons butter *or* margarine, melted
  Green pepper rings (optional)

In medium mixing bowl combine beaten egg, cream-style corn, shredded Swiss cheese, *half* of the cracker crumbs, milk, chopped onion, and pepper; mix well. Turn corn mixture into a 5×5×2-inch baking dish.

Toss the remaining cracker crumbs with the melted butter or margarine. Sprinkle over corn mixture. Bake in 350° oven about 30 minutes or till knife inserted halfway between center and edge comes out clean.

Let stand about 5 minutes before serving. Garnish with green pepper rings, if desired. Makes 2 servings.

†See page 3 for directions.

Breads

Funnel Cakes *add a new twist to breakfast. Pour the pancake-like batter through a funnel, moving it in a circular motion, then fry till crisp.*

Funnel Cakes

2 beaten eggs
1½ cups milk
2 cups all-purpose flour
1 teaspoon baking powder
½ teaspoon salt
2 cups cooking oil
   Powdered sugar
   Maple-flavored syrup
   (optional)

For batter, in mixing bowl combine beaten eggs and milk. Stir together flour, baking powder, and salt. Add to egg mixture; beat smooth with rotary beater.

In an 8-inch skillet heat cooking oil to 360°. Using a finger to cover the bottom opening of a funnel with a ½-inch spout (inside diameter), pour a generous ½ cup of batter into funnel. Remove finger and release batter into the hot oil, moving funnel in a circular motion to form a spiral. Fry about 2½ minutes or till golden brown. Using 2 wide metal spatulas, turn cake carefully. Cook about 1 minute more.

Drain on paper toweling; sprinkle with powdered sugar. Repeat with remaining batter. Serve cakes warm with maple-flavored syrup, if desired. Makes 4 or 5 cakes.

Streusel Coffee Cake

⅓ cup granulated sugar
¼ cup butter *or* margarine
1 egg
½ teaspoon finely shredded lemon peel
¼ teaspoon vanilla
¾ cup all-purpose flour
1 teaspoon baking powder
¼ teaspoon salt
3 tablespoons milk
¼ cup packed brown sugar
¼ cup all-purpose flour
¼ teaspoon ground cinnamon
2 tablespoons butter *or* margarine
2 tablespoons chopped walnuts

In small mixer bowl thoroughly cream granulated sugar and ¼ cup butter or margarine with electric mixer. Beat in egg, lemon peel, and vanilla. Stir together ¾ cup flour, baking powder, and salt. Stir into creamed mixture alternately with milk. Turn into greased and floured 6½×6½×2-inch baking dish.

Combine brown sugar, ¼ cup flour, and cinnamon; cut in 2 tablespoons butter or margarine till crumbly. Stir in walnuts. Sprinkle the brown sugar mixture over batter. Bake in 350° oven for 30 to 35 minutes. Makes 1 small coffee cake.

Bran Muffins

¾ cup whole bran cereal
½ cup buttermilk*
½ cup all-purpose flour
3 tablespoons brown sugar
1 teaspoon baking powder
¼ teaspoon baking soda
¼ teaspoon salt
1 egg
2 tablespoons cooking oil
⅓ cup raisins *or* snipped pitted dates (optional)

Combine bran cereal and buttermilk; let stand about 3 minutes or till liquid is absorbed. In mixing bowl stir together flour, sugar, baking powder, soda, and salt. Beat together bran mixture, egg, and oil; add to dry ingredients, stirring just till moistened. (Batter will be thick.) Fold in raisins or dates, if desired. Fill paper-lined muffin pans ⅔ full. Bake in 400° oven for 20 to 25 minutes. Makes 5 or 6 muffins.

If you don't have buttermilk, substitute 1½ teaspoons lemon juice or vinegar combined with enough whole milk to make ½ cup. Let stand 5 minutes.

Dill Bread

3 tablespoons butter *or* margarine, softened
1 teaspoon lemon juice
¼ teaspoon dried dillweed
4 slices French bread

In small mixing bowl combine butter or margarine, lemon juice, and dillweed; set aside.

Place bread slices on a baking sheet. Broil about 4 inches from heat for 1 to 2 minutes or till golden brown. Turn bread and spread the butter mixture on untoasted side of each bread slice. Broil 1 to 2 minutes more or till golden brown. Makes 2 servings. (Adaptable for one.)†

Caramel Upside-Down Muffins

1 tablespoon butter *or* margarine
2 tablespoons brown sugar
1 teaspoon light corn syrup *or* maple-flavored syrup
1 teaspoon water
2 tablespoons chopped pecans
¾ cup all-purpose flour
2 tablespoons granulated sugar
1¼ teaspoons baking powder
¼ teaspoon salt
1 beaten egg
2 tablespoons milk
1 tablespoon cooking oil

For caramel topping, in small saucepan melt butter or margarine. Stir in brown sugar, corn syrup or maple-flavored syrup, and water. Heat till blended; *do not boil.* Divide caramel topping among 6 muffin pans. Sprinkle pecans atop caramel topping.

In mixing bowl stir together flour, granulated sugar, baking powder, and salt. Combine egg, milk, and cooking oil. Add all at once to dry ingredients, stirring just till moistened. Divide mixture among the 6 prepared muffin pans. Bake in 400° oven for 13 to 14 minutes or till golden brown.

Immediately loosen sides and invert onto a plate. Drizzle caramel topping over muffins. Serve warm. Makes 6 muffins.

†See page 3 for directions.

Flaky Orange Pan Biscuits

½ cup all-purpose flour
1 teaspoon baking powder
½ teaspoon finely shredded orange peel
⅛ teaspoon salt
⅛ teaspoon cream of tartar
2 tablespoons shortening
3 tablespoons milk
1 tablespoon butter *or* margarine, melted
1½ teaspoons sugar
⅛ teaspoon ground nutmeg
   Butter *or* margarine (optional)

In mixing bowl stir together flour, baking powder, shredded orange peel, salt, and cream of tartar. Cut in shortening till mixture resembles coarse crumbs. Using a wooden spoon, make a well in center of flour mixture. Add milk all at once. Stir just till mixture clings together.

Divide dough into 4 pieces. With lightly floured hands, form each piece into a ball. Roll in melted butter or margarine; place in a 9-inch pie plate, spacing evenly. Combine sugar and nutmeg; sprinkle over dough. Bake in 450° oven about 15 minutes or till biscuits are golden brown. Serve warm with butter or margarine, if desired. Makes 4 biscuits.

Honey-Whole Wheat Bread

1 cup whole wheat flour
¾ to 1 cup all-purpose flour
2 tablespoons nonfat dry milk powder
1 package active dry yeast
1 teaspoon salt
¾ cup water
1 tablespoon honey *or* brown sugar
1 tablespoon cooking oil

In mixer bowl combine *½ cup* of the whole wheat flour, *½ cup* of the all-purpose flour, dry milk powder, yeast, and salt. In saucepan heat water, honey or brown sugar, and cooking oil just till warm (115°-120°). Add to dry mixture in mixer bowl. Beat at low speed of electric mixer for ½ minute, scraping sides of bowl constantly. Beat 3 minutes at high speed. By hand, stir in remaining whole wheat flour and enough of the remaining all-purpose flour to make a moderately stiff dough.

Turn out onto lightly floured surface and knead till smooth and elastic (about 3 minutes). Shape into a ball. Place in lightly greased bowl, turning once to grease surface. Cover and let rise in warm place till double (45 to 60 minutes).

Punch down; turn out onto lightly floured surface. Cover; let rest 10 minutes. Shape into a loaf. Place in greased 7½×3½×2-inch loaf pan. Cover and let rise in warm place till double (30 to 45 minutes). Bake in 375° oven for 25 to 30 minutes, covering with foil after 15 minutes. Makes 1 small loaf.

Individual Parmesan Loaves

2 pieces frozen white hamburger bun dough*
Shortening
2 tablespoons grated parmesan cheese
Cornmeal
Butter *or* margarine (optional)

Rub frozen buns with shortening. Thaw dough about 1½ hours at room temperature. Shape each piece into a miniature loaf about 4×1¼ inches. Brush lightly with cold water. Roll sides and top of each loaf in some of the parmesan cheese. Sprinkle a greased baking sheet with cornmeal. Place cheese-covered loaves on baking sheet. Let rise in warm place till almost double (about 30 minutes).

Place a shallow pan on lower oven rack; fill pan with boiling water. Sprinkle the top of each loaf with cold water, then sprinkle each with the remaining parmesan cheese, pressing cheese on lightly. Bake in 350° oven for 25 to 30 minutes or till golden brown. Serve warm with butter or margarine, if desired. Makes 2 individual loaves.

For sandwich-size individual loaves, use 3 pieces of dough. Shape into 4½×1¼-inch loaves, using 1½ pieces for each loaf.

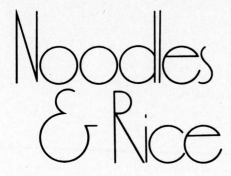

Noodles & Rice

Fettucini Alfredo

3 tablespoons grated parmesan
  or romano cheese
2 tablespoons whipping cream
1 tablespoon butter, melted
2 ounces fettucini *or* linguini
1 2½-ounce jar whole
  mushrooms, heated and
  drained

Combine cheese, whipping cream, and melted butter. Cook fettucini or linguini in boiling salted water about 8 minutes or till just tender. Drain.

Transfer fettucini or linguini to warm serving bowl. Add cheese mixture; toss to coat pasta. Stir in mushrooms. Season to taste with pepper. Serve immediately. Pass additional grated parmesan or romano cheese, if desired. Makes 2 servings.

To cook pasta, *fill a large saucepan with 1 quart cold water and 1 teaspoon salt for each 2 to 3 ounces pasta. Bring water to a rolling boil.*

Add 2 teaspoons cooking oil to water to prevent pasta from sticking together. Return water to a vigorous boil and add pasta.

Cook, uncovered, stirring at the start to prevent sticking. Begin taste-testing after 3 or 4 minutes to determine doneness. Cook pasta till tender yet firm to the tooth (al dente). Drain at once; do not rinse. Serve piping hot.

Hungarian Noodle Bake

1½ cups medium noodles
 2 tablespoons thinly sliced
   green onion
 1 small clove garlic, minced
 1 tablespoon butter *or*
   margarine
 ½ cup cream-style cottage
   cheese
 ¼ cup dairy sour cream
 ¼ teaspoon poppy seed
 ¼ teaspoon worcestershire
   sauce
 ⅛ teaspoon salt
   Dash pepper
   Dash bottled hot pepper
   sauce
 1 tablespoon grated
   parmesan cheese

Cook noodles in a large amount of boiling salted water about 8 minutes or just till tender; drain. Meanwhile, cook green onion and garlic in butter or margarine till onion is tender but not brown. Combine noodles, onion mixture, cottage cheese, dairy sour cream, poppy seed, worcestershire sauce, salt, pepper, and hot pepper sauce.

Turn noodle mixture into a greased 6½×6½×2-inch baking dish. Bake in 350° oven about 20 minutes. Sprinkle with parmesan cheese. Makes 2 servings.

Rice extravaganza

For **Fluffy Rice,** in 1-quart saucepan combine 1 cup cold water, ½ cup long grain rice, and ½ teaspoon salt. *Cover with tight-fitting lid. Bring to a rolling boil. Reduce heat to low and continue cooking for 14 minutes (do not lift cover). Remove from heat. Let* stand, covered, for 10 minutes. Makes 2 servings (1½ cups cooked rice total). (Adaptable for one serving.)†

Test for doneness: Pinch grains of rice between thumb and forefinger. The rice is done if there is no hard core.

For **Oven Rice,** in 1-quart casserole stir 2 teaspoons butter or margarine *into 1 cup* boiling water. *Stir in ½ cup long grain rice and ½ teaspoon salt. Cover and bake in 350° oven about 35 minutes or till rice is tender, fluffing with fork after 15 minutes. Makes 2 servings (1½ cups cooked rice total).*

Curried Rice

Prepare **Fluffy Rice** as directed above, *except* use ⅔ cup cold *water* and ⅓ cup long grain *rice;* add 2 tablespoons thinly sliced *celery,* 1 teaspoon instant *beef bouillon granules,* and 1 teaspoon *curry powder.*

Just before serving, add 2 tablespoons coarsely chopped *cashews* to hot cooked rice. Toss gently.

Parslied Rice Amandine

Prepare **Fluffy Rice** as directed above. Just before serving, stir 1 tablespoon snipped *parsley* into hot cooked rice. Sprinkle with 1 tablespoon chopped toasted *almonds.*

Confetti Rice

Prepare **Fluffy Rice** as directed above, *except* use ⅔ cup cold *water* and ⅓ cup long grain *rice.*

Meanwhile, cook ½ cup frozen *mixed vegetables* according to package directions; drain. Add cooked vegetables; 2 *cherry tomatoes,* quartered; and ⅛ teaspoon dried *dillweed* to hot cooked rice. Toss gently.

Spanish-Style Rice

Curried Rice

Browned Rice Pilaf

⅓ cup long grain rice
1 tablespoon butter
⅔ cup cold water
2 teaspoons instant chicken
  bouillon granules
½ teaspoon dried parsley
  flakes
¼ teaspoon minced dried onion
⅛ teaspoon garlic salt
⅛ teaspoon dried tarragon,
  crushed
⅛ teaspoon dried basil,
  crushed
⅛ teaspoon paprika
1 2-ounce can mushroom
  stems and pieces

In medium skillet cook rice in butter about 4 minutes or till golden brown, stirring frequently. Add water, bouillon granules, parsley, onion, garlic salt, tarragon, basil, and paprika. Drain mushrooms; stir into rice mixture. Bring to boiling; reduce heat. Cover and simmer for 20 to 25 minutes or till rice is tender. Makes 2 servings.

Spanish-Style Rice

3 tablespoons chopped green
  pepper
2 tablespoons chopped onion
1 small clove garlic, minced
1 tablespoon cooking oil
⅔ cup cold water
⅓ cup long grain rice
1 cup chopped peeled tomato
½ teaspoon salt
½ teaspoon instant chicken
  bouillon granules
  Dash bottled hot pepper
  sauce

In skillet cook green pepper, onion, and garlic in hot oil about 5 minutes or till tender. Add water and rice; stir in tomato, salt, bouillon granules, and hot pepper sauce. Bring to boiling; reduce heat. Cover and simmer about 20 minutes or till rice is tender. Makes 2 servings.

Wild Rice with Mushrooms

¼ cup wild rice
⅔ cup cold water
½ teaspoon instant chicken
  bouillon granules
1 slice bacon, cut up
¼ cup thinly sliced fresh
  mushrooms
1 tablespoon thinly sliced
  green onion
  Dash dried thyme, crushed
  Snipped parsley

Run cold water over rice in a strainer for 1 to 2 minutes, lifting rice with fingers. In saucepan combine rice, ⅔ cup water, and bouillon granules. Bring to boiling; reduce heat. Cover and simmer for 40 to 50 minutes or till rice is tender.

Meanwhile, in saucepan cook bacon till partially cooked. Add mushrooms, green onion, and thyme. Continue cooking till bacon is crisp and mushrooms are tender. Drain off fat. Add vegetables to cooked rice; toss gently. Season to taste with salt and pepper. Sprinkle with parsley. Makes 2 servings.

†See page 3 for directions.

Wild Rice with Mushrooms

Confetti Rice

DESSERTS

Peppermint Baked Alaskas
(see recipe, page 80)

Spiced Summer Fruit Dessert

Spiced Summer Fruit Dessert

2 tablespoons honey
1½ teaspoons lemon juice
½ teaspoon finely shredded orange peel
⅛ teaspoon ground cinnamon
1 orange, peeled and sectioned
½ cup fresh blueberries
½ cup halved seedless green grapes
½ cup halved strawberries
Toasted shredded *or* flaked coconut

Combine honey, lemon juice, orange peel, and cinnamon. Drizzle over orange sections in a bowl. Cover and chill several hours or overnight.

Shortly before serving, chill blueberries, green grapes, and strawberries. To serve, drain orange sections, reserving the liquid. Arrange orange sections, blueberries, green grapes, and strawberries in 2 individual dessert dishes. Drizzle the reserved liquid over fruit mixture. Sprinkle with toasted shredded or flaked coconut. Serves 2.

Coffee Cheesecakes

¼ cup crushed vanilla wafers (6 wafers)
2 teaspoons butter *or* margarine, melted
1 teaspoon sugar
1 egg white
2 tablespoons sugar
1 3-ounce package cream cheese, softened
1 tablespoon coffee liqueur

Combine vanilla wafers, melted butter or margarine, and 1 teaspoon sugar. Press into bottom of two 6-ounce custard cups.

In small mixing bowl beat egg white to soft peaks. Gradually add 2 tablespoons sugar, beating till stiff peaks form. Beat together softened cream cheese and coffee liqueur. Fold half of the egg white mixture into the cream cheese mixture. Return to remaining egg white mixture in mixing bowl.

Fill the prepared custard cups with egg white-cream cheese mixture. Bake in 350° oven for 15 minutes. (Cakes will puff, then fall when removed from oven.) Cool cakes in cups. Loosen sides of each cake with a knife and invert onto serving plate. Cover and chill.

To serve, drizzle with additional coffee liqueur, if desired. Makes 2 servings.

Peppermint Baked Alaskas

(pictured on page 78)

1 square (1 ounce)
    unsweetened chocolate,
    cut up
½ of a 5⅓-ounce can (⅓ cup)
    evaporated milk
½ cup sugar
1 tablespoon butter *or*
    margarine
½ teaspoon vanilla
2 cake dessert cups
    Peppermint ice cream
2 egg whites
½ teaspoon vanilla
¼ teaspoon cream of tartar
¼ cup sugar

For fudge sauce, in small saucepan combine chocolate and evaporated milk. Cook and stir over low heat about 7 minutes or till chocolate is melted. Stir in ½ cup sugar and butter or margarine. Cook and stir over medium heat for 3 to 4 minutes or till slightly thickened. Stir in ½ teaspoon vanilla. Cool.

Place cake cups on plate. Fill centers with some of the fudge sauce; freeze. Scoop out 2 large balls of peppermint ice cream; place 1 ball atop each cake cup. Using a spoon, scoop out a shallow indentation on top each ice cream ball. Fill hollow with additional fudge sauce. (Store any remaining sauce for another use.) Cover cake cups; freeze firm.

At serving time, beat egg whites, ½ teaspoon vanilla, and cream of tartar to soft peaks. Gradually add ¼ cup sugar, beating till stiff peaks form. Transfer cake cups to baking sheet. Quickly spread with egg white mixture, sealing to edges of cakes and baking sheet all around. Swirl to make peaks. Sprinkle with crushed peppermint candies, if desired. Bake in 500° oven for 2 to 3 minutes or till lightly browned. Serve immediately. Makes 2 servings.

Saucy Orange Cobbler

2 tablespoons sugar
1 tablespoon cornstarch
½ cup water
¼ cup orange marmalade
2 tablespoons frozen orange
    juice concentrate
2 teaspoons butter *or*
    margarine
½ cup packaged biscuit mix
    Dash ground nutmeg
3 tablespoons milk
½ pint vanilla ice cream (1 cup)

For orange sauce, in small saucepan combine sugar and cornstarch. Blend in water, orange marmalade, and frozen orange juice concentrate. Cook, stirring constantly, till mixture is thickened and bubbly. Cook 1 minute longer. Stir in butter or margarine till melted. Keep hot.

In small mixing bowl combine biscuit mix and nutmeg. Add milk, stirring just till moistened. Pour hot orange sauce into 5×5×1½-inch baking dish. Immediately drop dough in 2 portions onto orange sauce. Bake in 350° oven for 20 to 25 minutes.

Spoon warm cobbler and orange sauce into 2 dessert dishes. Place vanilla ice cream atop each serving. Spoon some of the orange sauce over ice cream. Makes 2 servings.

Sunshine Fruit Parfaits

2 tablespoons frozen orange
    juice concentrate
1 tablespoon sugar
½ cup frozen whipped dessert
    topping, thawed
1 small orange, peeled,
    sectioned, and cut up
1 small banana, sliced
½ cup fresh *or* canned
    pineapple chunks
¼ cup flaked coconut

In small bowl combine orange juice concentrate and sugar; mix well. Fold in thawed whipped topping. In small bowl combine orange pieces, banana slices, and pineapple chunks.

In 2 parfait glasses alternately layer fruit mixture, flaked coconut, and whipped topping mixture. Chill. Garnish parfaits with fresh mint sprigs and additional flaked coconut, if desired. Makes 2 servings.

Chocolate Mousse

⅔ cup light cream
½ cup semisweet chocolate
    pieces
1 egg yolk
1 tablespoon orange liqueur
    Sweetened whipped cream

In small saucepan combine light cream and chocolate pieces. Heat and stir over medium-low heat just till boiling. Remove from heat. Beat together egg yolk and orange liqueur. Gradually stir about half of the hot mixture into egg yolk mixture; return to hot mixture in saucepan. Cook and stir 1 minute longer.

Pour chocolate mixture into 2 small soufflé dishes or dessert dishes. Cover and chill at least 2 hours. To serve, top with whipped cream. Makes 2 servings.

Round out a meal in style with cooling Sunshine Fruit Parfaits *or warm-from-the-oven* Saucy Orange Cobbler *and ice cream.*

Fresh Fruit Crisp

2 tablespoons quick-cooking
 rolled oats
2 tablespoons brown sugar
1 tablespoon all-purpose flour
1 tablespoon chopped pecans
 (optional)
⅛ teaspoon ground cinnamon
 Dash salt
 Dash ground nutmeg
1 tablespoon butter *or*
 margarine
2 cups sliced peeled peaches,
 apples, *or* pears
2 teaspoons granulated sugar
 Vanilla ice cream *or* light
 cream

In small mixing bowl combine
rolled oats, brown sugar, flour,
pecans, cinnamon, salt, and nutmeg. Cut in butter or margarine
till crumbly; set aside.

Place fresh peaches, apples, or
pears in two 1-cup casseroles.
Sprinkle with granulated sugar.
Sprinkle rolled oat mixture over
fruit. Bake in 350° oven about 40
minutes or till fruit is tender.
Serve warm with vanilla ice
cream or light cream. Makes 2
servings.

Microwave cooking directions:
Prepare rolled oat mixture as
above; set aside. Place peaches,
apples, or pears in two 1-cup
nonmetal casseroles. Sprinkle
with granulated sugar. Sprinkle
rolled oat mixture over fruit.

Cook, uncovered, in countertop
microwave oven on high power
about 3½ minutes or till fruit is
tender, turning casseroles twice.
Serve as above.

Deep-Dish Peach Pie

1 frozen patty shell
2 tablespoons brown sugar
1 teaspoon quick-cooking
 tapioca
¼ teaspoon finely shredded
 lemon peel (optional)
½ teaspoon lemon juice
⅛ teaspoon ground nutmeg
 Dash salt
1 16-ounce can peach slices,
 drained
2 teaspoons butter *or*
 margarine

Thaw patty shell for 1 hour at
room temperature or for 2 hours
in the refrigerator.

Combine brown sugar, tapioca, lemon peel, lemon juice, nutmeg, and salt. Add peaches and
mix gently. Let stand for 15 minutes. Turn into a 20-ounce round
casserole. Dot with butter.

Roll out patty shell to a 6-inch
circle. Cut slits so steam can es-
cape; flute edge. Place over filling. Bake in 400° oven for 25 to 30
minutes or till golden brown.
Serve warm with light cream, if
desired. Makes 2 servings.

Hot Fruit Compote

1 11-ounce can pineapple
 tidbits and mandarin
 orange sections, drained
1 banana, sliced
2 tablespoons port wine
1 tablespoon brown sugar
2 teaspoons butter *or*
 margarine
 Dash salt
 Dash ground cinnamon

Combine fruits, wine, brown
sugar, butter, salt, and cinnamon. Cook over low heat,
stirring occasionally, till mixture
is heated through. Makes 2
servings. (Adaptable for one.)†

Baked Date-Filled Apples

2 tablespoons snipped pitted
 dates
1 tablespoon brown sugar
1 tablespoon chopped walnuts
¼ teaspoon ground cinnamon
2 large baking apples, cored
¼ cup water
2 tablespoons brown sugar
 Light cream *or* vanilla ice
 cream

In small mixing bowl combine
dates, 1 tablespoon brown sugar,
walnuts, and cinnamon. Peel off
a strip around top of apples.
Place apples in 1-quart casserole;
fill centers of apples with date
mixture.

Stir together water and 2 tablespoons brown sugar; pour over
apples. Bake, covered, in 400°
oven for 35 to 45 minutes or till
apples are tender. Baste occasionally with the juices. Serve
warm with cream or vanilla ice
cream. Makes 2 servings.

Microwave cooking directions:
Prepare date mixture as above.
Peel off a strip around top of apples. Place apples in 1-quart nonmetal casserole; fill centers with
date mixture. Cook, covered with
waxed paper, in countertop microwave oven on high power
about 5 minutes or till apples are
almost tender, giving dish a half
turn twice.

Stir together water and 2 tablespoons brown sugar; pour over
apples. Micro-cook, covered, for 1
to 2 minutes more or till apples
are tender. Let stand about 15
minutes before serving. Serve as
above.

Butterscotch Crunch

4 teaspoons cornstarch
⅛ teaspoon salt
1 cup milk
1 slightly beaten egg yolk
¼ cup packed brown sugar
1 tablespoon butter *or*
　margarine
½ teaspoon vanilla
1 1⅛-ounce chocolate-coated
　English toffee bar
2 tablespoons toasted coconut

In small saucepan combine cornstarch and salt; stir in milk. Cook and stir till thickened and bubbly. Cook for 2 minutes more; remove from heat. Gradually stir about half the hot mixture into egg yolk; return to hot mixture. Cook and stir 1 to 2 minutes or till thickened. Remove from heat. Stir in brown sugar, butter or margarine, and vanilla. Cover surface with clear plastic wrap or waxed paper. Cool, then chill.

　Crush toffee bar. Combine crushed toffee and coconut. In 2 sherbet dishes alternately layer chilled pudding and coconut mixtures. Makes 2 servings.

Whipped Raspberry Topping

2 slices pound cake*
⅓ cup raspberry yogurt
⅓ cup frozen whipped dessert
　topping, thawed
½ teaspoon sugar

Place each slice of cake on a dessert plate. Combine yogurt, topping, and sugar; spoon atop cake. Makes about ⅔ cup topping.

　If using frozen pound cake, slice cake without thawing, then return remaining cake to freezer. Cake slices will thaw quickly.

Home-Style Rice Pudding

1 cup milk
¼ cup long grain rice
¼ cup raisins
2 tablespoons butter *or*
　margarine
1 beaten egg
1 cup milk
3 tablespoons sugar
½ teaspoon vanilla
¼ teaspoon salt
　Ground cinnamon *or* nutmeg
　Light cream

In heavy small saucepan bring 1 cup milk, long grain rice, and raisins to boiling; reduce heat. Cover and cook over very low heat for 15 to 17 minutes or till rice is tender. Remove saucepan from heat; stir in butter or margarine till melted.

　In mixing bowl combine beaten egg, 1 cup milk, sugar, vanilla, and salt. Gradually stir rice mixture into egg mixture. Turn into a 6½×6½×2-inch baking dish. Bake in 325° oven for 25 minutes. Stir; sprinkle with cinnamon or nutmeg. Bake about 10 minutes longer or till knife inserted off-center comes out clean. Serve rice pudding warm or chilled with light cream. Makes about 2½ cups pudding.

Hot Fudge-Rum Turtle Sundaes

¼ cup semisweet chocolate
　pieces
1 tablespoon milk
¼ cup tiny marshmallows
1 tablespoon light rum
　Vanilla ice cream
　Toasted pecan halves

In small saucepan combine semisweet chocolate pieces and milk. Cook and stir over low heat till chocolate is melted. Remove from heat. Add marshmallows and rum; stir till marshmallows are partially melted.

　Scoop servings of ice cream into 2 dessert dishes. Top with chocolate mixture, then pecans. Makes 2 servings.

Microwave cooking directions: In 1-cup glass measure combine semisweet chocolate pieces and milk. Cook, uncovered, in countertop microwave oven on high power about 1 minute or till chocolate is melted, stirring once. Stir in marshmallows and rum. Serve as above.

Frozen Strawberry Creme

1½ cups fresh strawberries
1 tablespoon sugar
½ pint strawberry ice cream
　(1 cup)
¼ cup dairy sour cream
1 tablespoon orange liqueur

Sprinkle strawberries with sugar. Chill about 1 hour. Stir ice cream just enough to soften. Fold in sour cream and liqueur. Freeze about 1 hour.

　Spoon berries into 2 dessert dishes. Dollop each serving with ice cream mixture. (Keep remaining mixture frozen to serve with other fresh fruits or angel cake.) Serves 2. (Adaptable for one.)†

†See page 3 for directions.

BEVERAGES & SNACKS

Beer and Cheese Dip

Brandy-Wine Cooler

1½ cups dry white wine, chilled
    Juice of 1 orange (about ⅓ cup)
¼ cup peach brandy, chilled
    Ice cubes
    Assorted fresh fruits: orange *or* peach wedges, apple slices, pineapple chunks, melon balls, *and/or* strawberries
    Mint sprigs

In a pitcher combine chilled white wine, orange juice, and peach brandy. Add ice cubes. (Or, pour the wine-brandy mixture over ice cubes in 2 glasses.)

    Garnish with desired fresh fruit and fresh mint sprigs. Makes 2 servings. (Adaptable for one.)†

Beer and Cheese Dip

1 cup finely shredded sharp cheddar cheese
1 tablespoon butter *or* margarine, softened
1 teaspoon prepared mustard
¼ teaspoon prepared horseradish
3 tablespoons beer*
    Raw vegetable dippers *or* assorted crackers

Have cheese at room temperature. In small mixer bowl combine cheese, butter, mustard, horseradish, and ⅛ teaspoon *pepper*. Heat beer just to boiling; immediately pour over cheese. Beat with electric mixer about 3 minutes or till smooth. Serve warm or chill, and then let stand at room temperature about 1 hour before serving. Top with snipped chives, if desired. Serve as a dip for vegetables or as a spread for crackers. Makes ½ cup.

    **If chilling dip, increase the beer to ¼ cup.*

†See page 3 for directions.

Brandy-Wine Cooler

Irish Coffee

1 teaspoon instant coffee
  crystals
½ to 1 teaspoon sugar
½ cup boiling water
2 tablespoons Irish whiskey
  Whipped cream

Heat an 8-ounce serving glass or mug by rinsing with boiling water. Place coffee crystals and sugar in glass or mug; stir in ½ cup boiling water. Stir in whiskey. Top with large dollop of whipped cream. Makes 1 serving.

Coffee Frosted

1 cup crushed ice
½ cup vanilla ice cream
¼ to ⅓ cup coffee liqueur
½ teaspoon instant coffee
  crystals

In blender container combine ice, ice cream, liqueur, and coffee crystals. Cover and blend at high speed about 20 seconds or till smooth. Pour into 2 chilled glasses. Makes 2 servings. (Adaptable for one.)†

Cherry Fizz

⅓ cup cherry preserves
2 teaspoons water
1 pint cherry-nut *or* vanilla ice
  cream (2 cups)
1 10-ounce bottle (1¼ cups)
  lemon-lime carbonated
  beverage, chilled

Combine cherry preserves and water; chill. Pour cherry mixture into 2 tall, chilled glasses. Add scoops of cherry-nut or vanilla ice cream. Fill with carbonated beverage, pouring slowly down sides of glasses. Makes 2 servings. (Adaptable for one.)†

Eggnog Royale

1¼ cups milk
1 tablespoon sugar
1 to 1½ teaspoons instant
  coffee crystals
  Dash salt
1 beaten egg yolk
1 egg white
1 tablespoon sugar
¼ teaspoon vanilla
  Ground nutmeg

In saucepan combine milk, 1 tablespoon sugar, coffee crystals, and salt. Heat through. Gradually stir about half the hot mixture into egg yolk; return to hot mixture. Cook over low heat for 1 to 2 minutes more. Beat egg white, 1 tablespoon sugar, and vanilla to soft peaks.

Heat 2 mugs by rinsing with boiling water. Pour warm milk mixture into mugs. Top with egg white mixture. Sprinkle with nutmeg. Makes 2 servings.

Pineapple-Orange Soda

  Orange sherbet
1 cup unsweetened pineapple
  juice, chilled
⅓ cup orange juice, chilled
  Few drops aromatic bitters
  (optional)
1 10-ounce bottle (1¼ cups)
  lemon-lime carbonated
  beverage, chilled

Place a small scoop sherbet in each of 2 chilled glasses. Combine pineapple juice, orange juice, and aromatic bitters.

Pour a small amount of juice mixture into each glass; stir to muddle sherbet. Add remaining juice mixture. Add another scoop sherbet. Fill glasses with carbonated beverage, pouring slowly down sides. Makes 2 servings. (Adaptable for one.)†

Frothy Grasshopper

2 tablespoons green crème de
  menthe
2 tablespoons white crème de
  cacao
1 cup vanilla ice cream
1 10-ounce bottle (1¼ cups)
  carbonated water, chilled

In each of 2 tall glasses combine 1 tablespoon crème de menthe, 1 tablespoon crème de cacao, and small amount of ice cream. Add ¼ cup carbonated water to each glass; stir to muddle ice cream. Add remaining carbonated water, then additional scoops of ice cream. Makes 2 servings. (Adaptable for one.)†

Orange Spiced Tea

1 cup orange-flavored
  breakfast drink powder
1 cup instant tea powder
1 3-ounce package
  sugar-sweetened
  lemonade mix
½ teaspoon ground cinnamon
¼ teaspoon ground cloves

Combine all the ingredients. Store in tightly covered container. Stir before using.

To use, place 1 rounded tablespoon mix into a mug. Fill with boiling *or* cold water. Stir to dissolve. Makes about 2 cups mix.

Pink Daiquiri

¼ cup light rum
2 tablespoons lime juice
1 tablespoon grenadine syrup
2 to 3 teaspoons sugar
  Crushed ice

Combine first 4 ingredients. Pour over ice in 2 glasses. Makes 2 servings. (Adaptable for one.)†

Spicy Hot Chocolate

2 tablespoons sugar
2 tablespoons unsweetened
    cocoa powder
2 inches stick cinnamon
2 whole cloves
¼ teaspoon grated orange
    peel
    Dash salt
3 tablespoons water
1½ cups milk

In small saucepan combine sugar, cocoa powder, cinnamon, cloves, orange peel, and salt. Blend in water. Bring to boiling, stirring constantly. Boil gently for 1 minute. Stir in milk; heat almost to boiling. *Do not boil.* Remove whole spices. Beat with rotary beater till frothy. Pour into 2 mugs or cups; sprinkle with ground nutmeg, if desired. Makes 2 servings. (Adaptable for one.)†

Frozen Chocolate Bananas

½ cup milk chocolate pieces *or*
    semisweet chocolate
    pieces
2 wooden sticks
1 large banana, halved
    crosswise
¼ cup chopped peanuts *or*
    flaked coconut

In heavy small skillet or saucepan, melt chocolate over very low heat, stirring constantly (do not add any liquid). Remove from heat. Insert wooden sticks into banana halves. Carefully spread chocolate over entire banana half, then roll immediately in peanuts or coconut. Place on waxed paper-lined, shallow baking pan or baking sheet. Freeze till firm. (If not eaten the same day, wrap snacks in moisture-vaporproof wrap and store in freezer.) Makes 2 snacks.

Pepper-Beef Appetizers

6 ounces beef sirloin steak, cut
    1 inch thick
1 2½-ounce jar whole
    mushrooms, drained
¼ cup dry red wine
2 tablespoons cooking oil
1 tablespoon vinegar
½ teaspoon sugar
½ teaspoon salt
½ teaspoon dried rosemary,
    crushed
⅛ teaspoon pepper
    Green pepper cut into 1-inch
    squares

Place steak on unheated rack in broiler pan. Broil about 3 inches from heat for 16 to 18 minutes or till medium-rare, turning once. Cool slightly. Cut meat into ¾-inch pieces, trimming off fat.

Place meat and mushrooms in plastic bag; set in shallow dish. For marinade combine wine, oil, vinegar, sugar, salt, rosemary, and pepper; pour over meat and mushrooms. Close bag, marinate for 3 to 4 hours or overnight in refrigerator, turning bag occasionally. Drain meat and mushrooms; discard marinade.

Serve as many appetizers as you need right now, and save the remaining ingredients for appetizers another time. To assemble each appetizer for immediate use, thread a piece of meat, green pepper square, and mushroom on a wooden pick. To store appetizers for later use, alternately thread the remaining meat and mushrooms on wooden picks. Wrap and freeze. Add green pepper squares before serving. Makes 12 appetizers.

†See page 3 for directions.

Try Frozen Chocolate Bananas on sticks, coated with crunchy peanuts or flaky coconut, for pleasurably handy snacking.

TIPS & TECHNIQUES

Planning and preparing meals

Meal planning guides

Delicious meals depend on a successful blend of flavors and textures. To add variety, serve a crisp food with a soft food, contrast a bland flavor with a zesty or tart food, balance a hot food with a cold accompaniment, accent a food that has little color with a bright garnish, and plan a light dessert with a hearty meal.

If you want to simplify a meal, cut down the number of selections by combining several types of food in one dish, such as a meat, macaroni, and vegetable casserole.

Pay attention to nutrition

For good health and good eating, plan daily meals that include dairy foods, fruits and vegetables, meats or other high-protein foods, and breads or pasta. But don't limit your selections. For instance, use milk in soups, sauces, and desserts as well as in beverages. Feature fruit as an appetizer or dessert. Include vegetables in main dish casseroles, salads, and sandwiches.

If you're too busy to prepare a full meal, use snacks as a nutritional supplement. Eat cheese instead of candy, or drink a milk shake instead of soda pop.

Food buying hints

Set aside a time to plan your meals for the week. This way you can save time shopping with a single trip to the store, and you can save time preparing food because everything you need will be on hand.

Scan newspaper ads for good food buys. Fresh fruits and vegetables "in season" will usually be of better quality and the best buy. To cut down meat costs, serve smaller portions (3 ounces of cooked meat is adequate); make the meat go further by using it in casseroles, soups, and main dish salads; and plan meals around high-protein foods other than meat.

When making your selections, consider the amount of food you're able to use and the storage space you have available. Shop for fresh fruits and vegetables in stores where they aren't prepackaged so you can buy the amount you need. Buy frozen vegetables in plastic bags. These vegetables separate easily when frozen so you can remove and cook just what's needed.

Creating meals for one

—Eggs and cheeses are great for single size entrées.

—Keep frozen fish on hand for quick meals. Cut a single-serving portion from the package of frozen fish and return the remainder to the freezer.

—Refer to the ideas on page 66 for single-serving salads.

—Combine fresh fruit with cheese for a simple and delicious dessert.

—Fill out a meal with delicatessen foods you don't have time to make for yourself.

—If you have freezer space, buy several cuts of meat in one shopping trip and freeze them in single-serving portions. Shape ground beef into patties before freezing. Wrap patties in clear plastic wrap or foil so you can use them one at a time.

—If a recipe makes two individual casseroles, assemble both and store one for later use. Cover the dish tightly and refrigerate up to 2 days. When you heat the casserole, allow an extra 5 to 10 minutes baking time. Or, freeze the extra casserole and use within 2 to 3 months. To reheat the casserole without thawing, almost double the baking time. (Or, thaw the casserole first, then bake an additional 5 to 10 minutes.)

—Prepare a two-serving recipe and store what's left for another meal. The recipe will make more food than you need for one, but not more than you can use readily.

—Serve leftover foods a different way the second time. For instance, have leftover rice pudding for breakfast. Carry extra stew in a wide-mouth vacuum bottle for a lunch-box lunch.

Preparation tips

—Before starting meal preparation, read all recipes completely and assemble the utensils and ingredients needed.

—When chopping a small amount of onion or green pepper for a recipe, chop the whole vegetable at one time, then store the excess for later use. Keep in a tightly covered container in the refrigerator for a few days. Or, freeze in recipe-size portions so you don't have to remeasure. Use frozen portions within 1 month.

—If you use cheese frequently in cooking, save time by shredding a quantity that will be used in a few days. Cover and store it in the refrigerator. You can sprinkle a little shredded cheese atop cooked dishes for an attractive garnish.

—Use your countertop oven for a variety of cooking tasks. Adjust recipe timings slightly if your oven tends to be faster or slower than a conventional oven.

—Use a mini-fryer to deep-fat fry small batches of food easily and economically. Size foods to fit, if necessary, and add only a few pieces at a time to avoid spattering. Allow a little space between pieces so they'll fry quickly and brown evenly.

—Fire up your hibachi when you want to grill small quantites of food outdoors.

Stocking your kitchen

Organizing your kitchen

Keeping your kitchen organized and orderly will save time. Place utensils and staples near the areas where they're used most often. Store seldom-used utensils and appliances in an out-of-the-way place and move frequently used items to handy locations. Organize canned goods and packaged mixes on shelves by types so you can find them quickly.

Selecting kitchen tools

Any cook who has never stocked a kitchen or who is trimming down on kitchen equipment faces the "how many pots and pans do I need?" dilemma. The following guidelines will help you decide how to stock your kitchen with the essentials:

—Choose pieces you can use for more than one job, such as freezer-to-oven-to-table baking dishes and casseroles, and oven-going skillets.

—Every saucepan and skillet should have a secure cover. Make sure that cover knobs and handles are made of materials that don't conduct heat.

—Look for seals of approval, standards, and testing on appliances. (Gas appliances should have the American Gas Association seal. Look for the Underwriters' Laboratory seal on all electrical equipment.)

Basic equipment

The equipment needed to prepare food can be broken down into four groups—preparation and cooking utensils, bakeware, top-of-the-range cookware, and equipment for food storage. The variety available can be overwhelming, but remember that it isn't necessary to have everything. Concentrate first on the small-scale equipment and basic utensils listed. They should adequately supply a kitchen. Purchase other less essential equipment as the need arises.

Preparation and cooking utensils: Set of mixing bowls; nested set of dry measuring cups; clear glass liquid measuring cup; set of standard measuring spoons; wooden spoons; rubber spatulas; flexible metal spatula; serrated knife for bread, tomatoes, and citrus; paring knife with 3-inch blade; utility knife with 6-inch blade; French cook's or chef's knife; vegetable peeler; meat mallet; long-handled fork; long-handled spoon; ladle; slotted spoon; pancake turner; tongs; kitchen scissors; bottle opener; can opener; rotary beater and/or electric mixer; potato masher; grater or shredder; small and large strainers; colander; kitchen timer; wooden or plastic cutting board; rolling pin with cover; pastry cloth; and pastry brush.

Bakeware: Baking sheet or jelly roll pan, wire cooling rack, 6-ounce custard cups, muffin pan, pie plate, loaf baking pan, individual covered casseroles, 1-quart covered casserole, 6½×6½×2-inch baking dish, square baking pan (8×8×2 inches), oblong baking dish (10×6×2 inches), roasting pan with rack, and meat thermometer.

Top-of-the-range cookware: Select 1- and 2-quart covered saucepans and a 4- to 6-quart covered kettle or Dutch oven. (When cooking, it's best to use about ⅔ of the pan's capacity.)

A 6- to 8-inch and a 10-inch covered skillet will fill most any need.

Food storage: For storing uncooked and cooked food, stock up on assorted refrigerator-freezer dishes, foil, clear plastic wrap, waxed paper, and assorted canisters.

Basic groceries

Most foods you buy are matters of preference, but there are some food staples you can't cook without. Buy these things in quantities you can use up within a reasonable period of time. When buying perishable foods, choose the form—fresh, canned, dried, or frozen—that best fits your needs and storage facilities. When you start to run low on an item, note it for your next shopping trip.

Keep these foods on hand: Sugar, all-purpose flour, salt, pepper, baking powder, baking soda, coffee and/or tea, shortening, cooking oil, butter and/or margarine, assorted herbs and spices, vanilla, unsweetened cocoa powder, mayonnaise and/or salad dressing, prepared mustard, worcestershire sauce, catsup, bread, cereals, pasta, eggs, meat, salad greens, vegetables, fruits, cheese, juices, and milk.

Using canned foods

Health life versus shelf life: The *health life* of canned foods (the length of time they're safe to eat) is extensive. That's because the food has been sterilized. So long as the seal stays airtight, the food won't spoil.

Processors usually say the *shelf life* of canned foods (the time the food tastes its best) is about one year. You don't need to toss the can after a year, but canned food loses some flavor and nutrients in prolonged storage.

Selecting canned foods: Avoid buying badly dented cans. They could develop a leak. Small dents on the body of a can generally are harmless, but reject a can with dented side seam or end seams, visible leaks, or swollen ends.

Storing canned foods: Keep canned foods in a cool (below 70°F.), dry, dark place. Discard any can that's very rusty.

Once opened, store the can, covered, in the refrigerator. You can keep food in its original can for up to two days. For longer storage, transfer food to covered glass or plastic container.

Storing food

Proper care and storage will keep food at its best. Refrigerate or freeze perishable foods as soon as possible. Once food is cooked, cover and refrigerate or freeze any leftovers promptly. Thaw frozen foods in the refrigerator or place them in a sealed bag under cold running water.

Meat, Poultry, Fish: Fresh meat and poultry wrapped in clear flexible packaging may be refrigerated as purchased. To freeze, remove the clear packaging and wrap tightly in moisture-vaporproof material. (Prepackaged meat and poultry can be frozen for 1 to 2 weeks without rewrapping.)

Refrigerate or freeze fresh fish wrapped in moisture-vaporproof material.

Fruits, Vegetables: Most fresh fruits and vegetables are best stored in the refrigerator crisper. Keep stable vegetables such as potatoes, dry onions, and root vegetables in a cool, well-ventilated place.

Dairy Products, Eggs: Store cheese, milk, and butter, tightly covered, in the refrigerator. Eggs keep best refrigerated in a covered container, preferably the egg carton.

FOOD	MAXIMUM STORAGE TIMES	
	Refrigerator (36°F. to 40°F.)	Freezer (0°F. or lower)
MEAT		
Beef	2 to 4 days	6 to 12 months
Pork	2 to 4 days	3 to 6 months
Ground Meats	1 to 2 days	3 months
Ham	7 days	2 months
Ham Slices	3 to 4 days	2 months
Bacon	5 to 7 days	1 month
Frankfurters	4 to 5 days	1 month
Fresh Pork Sausage	7 days	2 months
Smoked Sausage	3 to 7 days	do not freeze
Dry Sausage	2 to 3 weeks	do not freeze
Luncheon Meats	7 days	do not freeze
Lamb	2 to 4 days	6 to 9 months
Veal	2 to 4 days	6 to 9 months
Variety Meats	1 to 2 days	3 to 4 months
Cooked Meats	4 to 5 days	2 to 3 months
POULTRY		
Chicken	1 to 2 days	12 months
Chicken Pieces	1 to 2 days	6 months
Turkey	1 to 2 days	6 months
Cooked Poultry	1 to 2 days	1 month
FISH	1 to 2 days	6 months
CASSEROLES AND OTHER MAIN DISHES	2 days	2 to 3 months
SANDWICHES (Do not freeze sandwiches containing mayonnaise.)	1 day	2 weeks
BREADS	2 to 4 days at cool room temperature	2 months
COOKIES	3 to 5 days at cool room temperature	12 months
BUTTER	7 days	3 to 6 months

Index

Recipes for One

See page 3 for information on adapting recipes for one.

Tips

A–B

Anise Carrots............. 68
Appetizers, Pepper-Beef 87
Apple-Bean Bake 70
Apple-Sausage Curry........ 38
Avocado-Chicken Salad
  Amandine 59
Bacon-Tomato Muffins,
  Broiled 63
Bacon-Wrapped Stuffed
  Frank 41
Baked Date-Filled Apples.... 82
Baked Halibut Steaks 44
Baked Veal Parmesan 15
Barbecued Pork........... 29
Barbecue Recipes
  Barbecued Bass Steaks.... 44
  Beef Kabobs Burgundy.... 17
  Grilled Chinese Pork
    Tenderloin 30
  Ham Hawaiian 33
  Individual Clambakes..... 48
  Lemon Barbecued Steak... 17
  Skillet Fried Fish 45
  Spicy Barbecued Chicken 10
Basic Omelet.............. 52
Basic Pork Mixture 28
Bavarian Supper........... 19
Beef
  Bavarian Supper......... 19
  Beef in Olive-Tomato
    Sauce 20
  Beef Kabobs Burgundy.... 17
  Beef Short Rib Stew....... 18
  Beef Sirloin Three-Way
    Dinners 16
  Chef's Salad............ 56
  Garden Swiss Steak 20
  Lemon Barbecued Steak... 17
  Pot Roast Dinner 19

Beef (continued)
  Reuben Casserole........ 19
  Sautéed Liver and
    Vegetables 22
  Short Ribs with Limas..... 18
  Sirloin Salad Supreme 17
  Steak and Shrimp Creole.. 20
  Steak Bertrand.......... 19
  Steak-Lobster Dinner...... 15
  Steak Sandwiches with
    Mushrooms........... 62
  Sweet and Sour Liver
    Skewers 22
Beef, Ground
  Beef and Rice Espagnole .. 25
  Beefed-Up Peppers 24
  Burgers Stroganoff........ 24
  Chili for Two 25
  Herbed Spaghetti Sauce... 25
  Saucy Meatballs 22
  Scotch Meat Loaves 23
  Spanish Hamburger Soup 60
  Sproutburger 24
  Taco Salad 58
  Tangy Meat Loaf 23
Beer and Cheese Dip 85
Beer Rarebit Fondue....... 55
Berry-Fruit Salad......... 67
Beverages
  Brandy-Wine Cooler 85
  Cherry Fizz............. 86
  Coffee Frosted 86
  Eggnog Royale 86
  Frothy Grasshopper 86
  Irish Coffee............. 86
  Orange Spiced Tea....... 86
  Pineapple-Orange Soda... 86
  Pink Daiquiri 86
  Spicy Hot Chocolate 87
Bouillabaisse............. 46
Brandy-Wine Cooler....... 85
Bran Muffins 73
Breaded Fish Portions with
  Dill Sauce.............. 46
Breads
  Bran Muffins........... 73
  Caramel Upside-Down
    Muffins 73
  Dill Bread 73
  Flaky Orange Pan Biscuits 74
  Funnel Cakes........... 72
  Honey-Whole Wheat
    Bread 74
  Individual Parmesan
    Loaves............... 74
  Streusel Coffee Cake..... 73
Breakfast Omelet.......... 53
Broiled Apple-Stuffed
  Chicken 11

S

T-Z